I0035799

Dot

Money

www.DotMoneyBook.com

Eric Majors

www.EricMajors.com

Copyright © 2014 Eric Majors
All rights reserved.
ISBN: 0986291706
ISBN-13: 978-0986291708
www.DotMoneyBook.com

Published by The Write For Right Project
www.WriteForRight.com
The Right For Right Project is an international, humanitarian
sustainable business project
of the publishing division of Xt Blue, Inc.
that is funded by a combination of donations, products sales and
the financial support of Xt Blue, Inc.
www.XtBlue.com
Please support the goals and work of the
Write For Right Project to help all artists in the world by buying
products sponsored by the Write For Right Project
and making donations to the Write For Right Project at
www.WriteForRight.com

DEDICATION

I dedicate this book to my wife loving wife Lisa, my son Ian and my daughter Trinity and also to everyone in the world as we are all connected.

I wrote this book in the hope that the solutions provided within will be implemented or that a new set of equally compelling solutions will be discovered and implemented. My hope in presenting the ideas of this book is to simulate thinking and action that will help to unlock the true and positive potential of the entire human race and to help all people to live more happily.

CONTENTS

ACKNOWLEDGEMENTS

I acknowledge and praise God our creator from whom all good things flow and who allowed me to be alive, write this book and have all of the experiences of my life and to share life with others. I acknowledge and praise Jesus Christ for providing me with a role model that is loving, giving, caring and forgiving that accepts me with my faults and knows my true heart and intentions. Anything good that I have ever done and everything good that I do is only because of the patience, love, kindness and forgiveness that Jesus Christ continually asks from me. All that I have done wrong in my life is as a result of my own human nature and selfishness that I strive to manage every day and for which I thank Jesus for his forgiveness that keeps us all whole and new as we are continually challenged to overcome our own selfishness and forgive the selfishness of others. Through continual seeking of the Holy Spirit through an ongoing study of and relationship with Jesus Christ I do experience and understand true peace, love and fulfillment in all circumstances and pray that it never ends and that everyone comes to know the presence of God and experience it every day.

I acknowledge and thank my wife Lisa, my son Ian, my daughter Trinity all of whom also inspire me to be a better man and teach me about love every day and without their patience and support this book would not be possible.   I acknowledge and thank my mother Marcella and my brother Jeff Richfield and his family who have all supported me when I've needed it most. I would also like to acknowledge and thank my deceased father and brother, Tom and Steve respectively for the contributions that they made in my life (I miss you both).

I acknowledge my dear friend and colleague, Derick Smith from South Africa, who has supported my family and I and who took pains taking efforts to help me edit, implement and obtain a publisher for this book.

I also acknowledge Dr. Jim Harris from the United States, who inspired me to write a white paper that turned into this book, and to Dr. Rakesh Rajagopal from Hong Kong who believed in the concepts so much that he spearheaded the launch of an entire global business around the concepts of the book.

I acknowledge the great work of the Write For Right Project (WriteForRight.Com) and for selecting my works for publication. I encourage everyone who reads this book to please donate to Write For Right and purchase products produced by them so they can expand their great work to make the world a better place and to help people. Write For Right is creating opportunities for artists and writers like myself who have been released from prison to get jobs and have their works completed and published around the world as part of the "Write Now Project." Write For Right is helping people who are in prison and other disadvantaged groups of people all around the world to get the critical material and support needed for them to produce writings and works of art that improve the health and lives of everyone concerned and bring important messages to the people of the world.

I acknowledge all of my friends and associates who have supported me, forgiven me and given me a second chance in life and who appreciate my intentions.

I acknowledge all of the people who are working around the world to help unlock the utility of money for the future of the human race by developing virtual and community currencies, and the technology that will facilitate a new world where money works for people rather than only people working for money.

IMPORTANT UPDATE

As part of the process of Pre-Publication of this book advanced copies were sent for review to various people and organizations. As a result of the enthusiasm with which the concepts of the book were received, certain parties have actually started the implementation of one of the most important and powerful concepts of the book, which is a new global virtual currency named "Dot Money" after this book.

Thus, as you are reading this book, "Dot Money" is becoming a reality in which you and everyone else in the world can participate.

Since this new effort is designed and named from the concepts of my book (and because I also hold the Trade Name) I have been invited, and I accepted, to take up an offer to be one of several spokespersons for the Dot Money enterprise. I will continue to lend my support so as long as I feel that the organization stays true the values and goals that I outlined in my book. The goals and the ideas of Dot Money are too big to be owned by any single person and so I am happy to leave the implementation to a more qualified group of people and international organizations and just continue to promote the concepts. However, I am very excited and pleased to see the work being done, which has such great implications for all of the people of the world and future generations and I do hope it succeeds.

For more information about the actual implementation of "Dot Money" and how you can sign up and support the movement please visit:

www.DotMoney.Cash

For more information on other related efforts in which you might want to lend support please visit my website: **www.DotMoneyBook.com**

Introduction

The biggest problem in the world today is that too few people are spending too little time trying to think of potential solutions to problems and spending too much time repeating the question 'Well what can we do?' Using the question is an answer itself and an excuse to avoid trying to make the world a better place. No matter what your background is don't ever think that you are too unsophisticated to think of answers yourself. Don't ever divorce yourself from the responsibility of trying to solve the problems of our society.   Don't leave that responsibility to elected officials alone. Instead just try spending some time thinking of solutions and also ask others to do the same. You may be surprised what problems you end up solving and who else may find solutions. The most valuable commodity in the world is not gold, silver or some other precious substance. The only truly valuable commodity in the world is ideas that spring from the human mind. It is our human thinking from which the idea and measure of value itself is derived and from which countless ventures and inventions stem.

In this book I provide the framework of a new economy that can potentially end poverty, establish global economic stability and help each individual to realize their true potential as a human being. The framework that I present is based on the ideas of others as well as my own experiences from working in the financial markets and living life.

I provide practical methods to implement these ideas today, with or without the cooperation of any government. I believe that the implementation of the framework described in this book is going to take place sooner or later - it's really only a matter of time. Our global economic and monetary policies have nowhere else to go other than in a direction that more closely resembles my framework. Many refer to the concepts in this book as Star Trek economics, because they seem to overcome the problems of our monetary systems to achieve a future where:

- there is no poverty

- people are free to engage in the pursuit of happiness

- people don't have to do job that they don't like in order to make ends meet

Some people will think these ideas are crazy and go against everything they've been taught to believe. Other people besides me, such many highly respected scientists and economists from places including from the U.S. Federal Reserve, will think that it is crazy to continue on our current course and not implement a framework such as this.

The decision rests with you. Please enjoy this book.

Part 1
The Concept of Money

Many heavily utilized inventions throughout the history of the world have had a notable impact on the behavior of human beings. The first thing that most people think about when you mention life changing inventions are those that involve physical devices that reduces labor, save time or help to perform some or other task more efficiently. Popular inventions that most commonly come to mind are tangible items such as the lever, the wheel, the printing press, the airplane, the television, the telephone and the computer. However, there is another class of inventions that exist as intangibles and whose value are derived from, and depend on, human relationships, ideas, agreements, attitudes and behaviors. These intangible inventions include abstractions that are extraordinarily influential on the quality of human life. These intangible inventions sometimes change in implementation over time and often result in the fabrication of tangible items. Examples of intangible inventions include things such as works of art, poetry, music, philosophical and scientific works, economics, agreements, laws, corporations, governments and money.

Intangible inventions depend heavily on the relationships between people and the ideas and beliefs that they agree upon and share. These commonly held ideas and beliefs are referred to as conventions. Conventions underpin the very foundation and quality of human existence. For example, because the majority of people agree (by convention) that murder is wrong the human race persists. If the majority of people all choose to believe and agree that murder is necessary and desirable then the human race may very rapidly cease to exist.

The primary subject of this book is about one of the most powerful intangible inventions in the history of mankind, namely money. Money would serve no function in a world without human beings and its value depends on the agreements, laws, beliefs and behaviors of human beings.

An observer may fix the value of a tangible invention such as a single metal lever according to, for example, the physical composition and shape, the number of simultaneous users the device may accommodate and the limitations of the device in producing specific results over time.

On the other hand the value of the intangible invention known as money can vary wildly and its ability to yield an outcome is limited only by the conventions of human beings. For example, if the government were to create a law that says that one dollar could be redeemed for an ordinary 1 ounce stone of any shape or size then it's very likely that no one would be motivated to perform any amount of work for a dollar because 1 ounce stones are readily available for free. However, if the government passed a law that said that one dollar could be redeemed for one cow, then it is likely that the same dollar could be used to motivate people to produce a variety of work since cows are valuable and useful.

This book depends on your ability to understand the significance of this example. In the example of stone versus cow the value of the money is established by an agreement (in this case by force of law) between two or more people. It is fundamental to understand that the only reason that money has any value at all is because there are people who are willing to accept an amount of money in exchange for goods and services. A dollar is just a small piece of metal or paper but the fact that it can be traded for goods or services establishes it as a tool with value that depends on the perspective of those who use it.

In spite of what is repeatedly drilled into our minds by economists, political parties, stock brokers, bankers and even governments, the value of any currency is not based on gold or silver, any tangible or circumstance in the world other than the agreements between people. When the majority of people are led to believe, for whatever reason, that the value of one U.S. Dollar (USD) is worth 8/10ths of one British Pound Sterling (GBP) then so it manifests. However, if the governments agreed to fix their exchange rates, as they have done in the past, then the value of one USD per GBP could also be changed by force law.

Chapter 2: Money As A Tool

Money is nothing more than a tool that was created by us for our convenience. What results from the use of money is only as good or bad as the intentions of the users of money. The value of money itself is based on agreements between people and, because of this fact, new currencies can be created at any time out of anything by agreement.

I believe that the use and understanding of money as a tool is still in its evolutionary stages. Advances in science, medicine and economics are perceived by most people to have a net positive impact on the quality of the life of human beings. Of course advances in any of these areas can sometimes also be dangerous and even deadly. There are notable inventions of science that have also had dangerous and unforeseen side effects, such those that use radioactive materials. Radioactive materials are used frequently in medicine for example to take X-rays and to treat certain illnesses. Contrastingly, radioactive materials have, at times, accidently leaked from reactors, causing illness and death despite our best intentions. So, when we consider the implementation of economic systems as utilized by communist versus capitalist systems of government we see that economics is also a form of science that can have dangerous or beneficial effects on the human race.

The results of any economic systems can, at best, be hard to predict, particularly when governments have immoral intents. Proper implementation of the production of money is one of the keys to producing the most beneficial effects.

Based on my study of the history and the evolution of the economies of the world it is my opinion that we are essentially still operating economic systems that uphold principles of property rights and ownership that were popular during the medieval times and before. I believe that, just as science and medicine have made amazing leaps that have had many beneficial results for mankind, our economic systems are due for a major evolutionary step that will forever change how we value and use money as a tool.

As with many inventions, the use of money as a tool to improve the condition and evolution of mankind has not yet been fully exploited. In order to fully utilize the tool of money for the benefit of mankind I believe that it is necessary for most people reconsider their thinking about money itself. This thinking has come from a variety of sources including parents, economists, business interests and governments. There are many notable events throughout history of the world that are worth reviewing in order to help us overcome our preconditioned thinking about how money really works in our world today and how we perceive the value of money.   With this idea of breaking our preconditioned notions about money, let's have a brief look at the history of money.

Chapter 3: The Evolution of Money

History clearly demonstrates that the value of money is based on agreements between individuals and groups.   Because laws represent the agreements imposed by force on people by government, governments historically have exerted the greatest influence and control over the value of money. Governments have routinely been in charge of creating the physical manifestation of money including coins, dollar bills, credit and their electronic representations.

Virtually all cultures around the world have used some medium of exchange in order to facilitate trade between people since recorded history began. Some cultures, such as the American Indians relied much less on trade and more on understandings and agreements and thus in some ways their economies were arguably more sophisticated than our modern economies. Today the majority of cultures around the world rely heavily on money as a medium for trade and in most places money is a necessity for survival. In all cases where cultures made use of some form of money you will also find some kind of government or other mutual understanding between people that "governs" transactions in money and trade. To illustrate the role of government in establishing and regulating use and value of money, consider antique coins unearthed from historical excavations or currency that remains from some recently defunct government. What was once established to have specific value by some government now only has value for collectors of antiquities.

This book is not intended to provide an exhaustive history of money, but rather a macro overview that is necessary to help inspire the evolution and use of money in order to maximize the benefits of the invention of money. Thus, for the purposes of this book we will reduce our examination of money to three distinct users of money throughout history:

- those who used commodity money (including representative money), such as metals like gold, as a medium of exchange and
- those who used commodity money (including representative money) other than gold or metal as a medium of exchange and
- those who either had no need to create a monetary system or did not use gold as a medium of exchange (such as the Mayan's for whom gold was used for artistic and spiritual purposes)

Money Made Of Gold

Let's have a look at the use of gold as a form of money first. What makes gold so special after all? Why do we consider gold to be so valuable when the possession of gold is not necessary to sustain life? If we were to consider something that might genuinely have value why not consider fish or some kind of produce that can be eaten or used to sustain life?

According to the latest theories of historians and scientists on the origin of the use of gold as the most popular medium of trade, the following fundamental reasons emerge: human nature (possibly genetics), practical necessity and its scarcity.

The human nature argument for the use of gold has to do with our primordial past. The theory is that human beings are predisposed to be attracted to sparkly things, possibly because they resemble the images created by light reflecting off of the life sustaining and comforting view of water on a lake or a stream. So there is the idea that the desire for sparkly things is inherent in our DNA.

Gold does not tarnish, rust or disintegrate as do most other readily available metals. This ability of gold to withstand the test of time makes gold an obvious choice of metal for crafting gifts or art. Just look at the gold artwork found in the tombs of the famous mummies in Egypt. After simply cleaning the dust from these artifacts they still retain their original appearance. For the same reason gold is an excellent choice for representing value.

The argument that gold is scarce also makes it an attractive selection for use as a currency because it is not easy to find and thus can be controlled by governments. As an example that helps to illustrate how the scarcity of gold can contribute to its perceived value, consider the modern day use of printed paper money. In order for governments to make it difficult for people to counterfeit their paper currency most governments heavily protect their formulas and procedures for the creation of the paper and inks that are used to print paper money. If everyone knew how to make the paper, inks and printing plates, then it would be easy for anyone to simply print and spend their own counterfeit currency. In a similar way, because gold is not readily available the supply and use of gold to make coins can be controlled by the government in the same way that specific paper used for money is guarded by government. It is interesting to note that one of the primary functions of government is also to protect and segregate property, including land and mineral rights.

In order to use gold to make coins for currency one must first obtain gold. This is one reason why countries have gone to war and why gold has historically been used to measure the value of the government of a country. Although it is no longer true today, when the treasury of a government ran out of gold, so did the perceived value of the government itself.

One of my favorite stories about money and gold comes from the New Testament of the Bible. When Jesus Christ was asked if people should pay taxes Christ responded by asking whose face appears on a coin. When the priests answered "Caesar's face" Jesus replied, "Then give to Creaser what belongs to Caesar." I love this profound and genius illustration that cuts right to the very foundation of money itself. Imagine if we took what Jesus advised and gave all of the money that was printed by the government (our Caesar) back to the very same government that printed it. Imagine what would happen. The money would be worthless no matter what it was made of. The government would cease to function because it would not be able to pay anyone with anything of any value because no-one would be using money for anything other than sending it back to Caesar. Soldiers would not work for money that people did not accept.

Some people speculate that if citizens used and valued a different currency to that issued by their home country then their government might lose power and authority. In practice this problem is easily overcome by the fact that any government can use the force of law to regulate the value and use of external currencies within their own boarders and thus prevent their own currency from losing value. This is one reason why most modern governments do not restrict the use of foreign currencies, new virtual currencies and barter trade to effect financial transactions within their borders. A good example is Zimbabwe, which allows the use of U.S. Dollars instead of their own currency, because the Zimbabwean Dollar lost all value in the global market.

We have examined some theories about why gold was considered the most popular form of money in history. Even though we can all acknowledge that none of us actually needs gold in order to sustain life we can also acknowledge that much of the perceived value of gold comes simply from the historical use and thinking about gold that still persists in our minds today. Gold remains valuable to us for the simple fact that we have all come to believe and agree that gold is valuable. Gold is rare and gold does have a price as a commodity. It is used in many objects that are considered essential today such as computers and cell phones. However, outside of the value of gold as a commodity, we have no basis for the value of gold other than our mutual acceptance and agreement that "gold should be held as precious and valuable." The simple fact is that gold is not essential to human life and its value as a commodity is influenced by so many forces that it may have been and may continue to be overvalued.

Something Other Than Gold As Money

Let's consider some societies that have used something other than gold as currencies. Coins made of metal other than gold have also been used as currencies by some countries because of the rarity of gold. Paper bills backed by precious metals have also been used out of convenience allowing people to carry a paper bill that can be redeemed for gold rather than having to carry heavy loads of gold or other metals used as currencies. These kinds of paper and coin currencies that can be redeemed for some store of a precious commodity are known as *Representative Money*. However, there are a variety of things that have been used as (or like) money by various cultures throughout history, including sea shells. Sea shells were used as currency by Native Americans in California as described in the historical records of the Europeans who first made contact with them. Items such as salt were used by early Romans, peppercorns were used by Attila the Hun, and in Africa some cultures still use bottle caps. In some modern prisons sacks of mackerel are used as currencies. Beaver pelts were often used to facilitate trade between Europeans and Native Americans and they were one of the few things that both agreed were highly valuable. When Argentina ran out of coins in 2008 people used tootsie rolls or other small candies instead.

Again, in order to really bring home the concept of the value of currency, consider the buying power in today's market for some currencies of antiquity, such as Rome and Greece. Consider currencies like the former Dinar of the defunct government of Saddam Hussein in Iraq. The Dinar was once valuable but now the bills are simply pieces of paper. Think of the buying power of currencies that devalued with poor governmental policies, such as Zimbabwean Dollars or Weimer Deutschmarks. Their buying power is zero, and their worth depends solely on their value to collectors of novelty items or antiques. Certainly none of the governments of the world value any of these currencies in facilitating trade. What was once valuable as a currency is no longer perceived as valuable by anyone even where some of the governments that once backed the currencies still exist.

For the purposes of debate it is only necessary to acknowledge that things such as shells have been used for money by cultures of the past. This fact proves the point that money is a tool that is designed for use by us and depends on agreements between people. If something as common as shells have been successfully used in the past as a means of trade then isn't the value of money itself actually in the minds of the users of the money? What more proof does one need?

Those Who Used No Money

It is important to remember that there have been cultures present and past, such as the Native Americans of old, the Hadza in Africa today and others, who still do not use money for one reason or another. The history of Native American money is a fascinating one. Their use of money was not widespread prior to contact with Europeans. The European use of money was deeply entrenched by the time they encountered the Native Americans.

Among the currencies used by Native Americans was "wampum", which is a sea shell that is the most famous form of their currency that is remembered today. The wampum eventually fell into disuse, initially among the colonists, because of inflation. Wampum was not difficult to "harvest" from the oceans and was perceived as worthless as time went by. Genuine wampum is valuable today as an artifact, but is not used for purchases.

Many Native Americans had quite sophisticated forms of trade and currency, whereas other tribes, such as the Inca in Peru, managed to develop a complex and advanced civilization without money. Even where money was used by the Native Americans there was a consciousness about money and property that was, in most cases, radically different from our modern thinking, and, arguably, more sophisticated. At the core of Native American belief was the idea that everything in the world was provided by The Creator (God) for use by everyone. In general most Native American's did not hold that property and land was to be divided up for individual ownership. The very idea that land could be owned by an individual was as silly as the idea that someone could own the air that we breathe or the sunlight that shines on us. Obviously the European system of property rights and ownership could not co-exist with the culture of the Native Americans.

It can be argued that the satisfaction and levels of happiness and mental health of many cultures that did not use money appeared to be quite high as documented by many historical records. These include the writings of Ben Franklin, who wrote about the American Indians:

"The Indian Men when young are Hunters and Warriors; when old, Counselors; for all their Government is by Counsel of the Sages; there is no Force, there are no Prisons, no Officers to compel Obedience, or inflict Punishment.—Hence they generally study Oratory; the best Speaker having the most Influence. The Indian Women till the Ground, dress the Food, nurse and bring up the Children, and preserve and hand down to Posterity the Memory of public Transactions. These

Employments of Men and Women are accounted natural and honorable, Having few artificial Wants, they have abundance of Leisure for Improvement by Conversation."

These levels of fulfillment of people from cultures who did not use money appeared to be remarkably high in spite of the perceived lack of sophistication of their science and medicine. The lifestyles of the Native Americans seemed more conducive to human health and life than the lifestyle experienced by the majority of citizens in our modern global economy, where our thinking and use of money and property is based on European (and older) ideas and systems.

When we closely examine the history of cultures where money was not present, the appreciation of life and engagement with intellectual and spiritual values appears to be more prominent. This eventually begs the inquiry as to whether or not we may be missing something in the quality of our lives because of our exposure, use and dependency on our modern economic and monetary systems. Take for example this account as told to Ben Franklin by an Indian when comparing our western manners, which appear to be inspired by love of money, to the manners of Indian people who had not yet been indoctrinated into the European way of thinking. Based on this text it appears that European standards of wealth (that tend to persist today around the world) are typically measured by amounts of money rather than in virtues such as freedom in life, abundance of time, happiness, caring and compassion for others, which really produces a good quality of life:

"You know our Practice. If a white Man in travelling

thro' our Country, enters one of our Cabins, we all treat him as I treat you; we dry him if he is wet, we warm him if he is cold, we give him Meat and Drinks that he may allay his Thirst and Hunger, and spread soft Furs for him to rest and sleep on: We demand nothing in return. But if I go into a white Man's House at Albany, and ask for Victuals and Drink, they say, where is your Money? And if I have none; they say, Get out you Indian Dog. You see they have not yet learnt those little Good Things, that we need no Meetings to be instructed in, because our Mothers taught them to us when we were Children..."

It is clear from this example (and many others) that one of the most significant negative side effects for users of money is the tendency to become more selfish and less sensitive to the needs of others. Another undesirable side effect of the use of money is that people tend to associate and store the perceived value of their lives within money, and thus mistakenly use money as a measure of their freedom, happiness and security. For example, rather than measuring the quality of life based on the quality of relationships, users of money will often measure the quality of their lives based on their perceived ability to create good relationships by using money as a tool. Thus the idea of the happiness derived from good relationships becomes something that can be stored in money rather than realized through action and experience.

While there is obviously great utility in using money as a tool it is instructive for us to acknowledge the obvious pitfalls associated with the use of money as demonstrated through experience and historical records as we have done.

These pitfalls are highlighted when compared to cultures that have not used money.

The Native American way of life involved fulfillment and happiness through their appreciation of and relationships between themselves and the naturally occurring world around them. In contrast historical records of the most influential Europeans indicate that the naturally occurring environment was something that needed to be tamed and crafted to suit a particular style of life. Even to this day the prevailing measure of happiness and wealth in Western and European cultures is often related directly to access to money and ownership of property. Again, the differences in thinking between the first European settlers/conquerors and the American Natives can be seen very clearly by examples such as the telling remarks recorded in history in regards to U.S. policy on [American] Indian affairs.

In 1887, J.D.C. Atkins, the U.S. Commissioner of Indian Affairs speaking on the allotment act to segregate the land of the Indians within their own reservation forcing the assignment of parcels of land to specific individual Indians against their will famously urged that *"[the Indian] must be imbued with the exalting egotism of American civilization so that he will say 'I' instead of 'We' and 'This is mine' instead of 'This is ours.'"* They strongly encouraged Native men to go forth and participate in a modern and fully competitive market economy: *"We must make the Indian more intelligently selfish. . . . By acquiring property, man puts forth his personality and lays hold of matter by his own thought and will."*

Speaking of the differences between Native

Americans and the invaders of their territories Chief Seattle said simply, *"The difference is in our hearts."* And most poignantly Chief Seattle wrote to the American Government in the 1800's:

"The President in Washington sends word that he wishes to buy our land. But how can you buy or sell the sky? The land? The idea is strange to us. If we do not own the freshness of the air and the sparkle of the water, how can you buy them? Every part of the earth is sacred to my people. Every shining pine needle, every sandy shore, every mist in the dark woods, every meadow, every humming insect. All are holy in the memory and experience of my people. This we know: the earth does not belong to man, man belongs to the earth. All things are connected like the blood that unites us all. Man did not weave the web of life, he is merely a strand in it. Whatever he does to the web, he does to himself. One thing we know: our God is also your God. The earth is precious to him and to harm the earth is to heap contempt on its creator. ... When the last red man has vanished with this wilderness, and his memory is only the shadow of a cloud moving across the prairie, will these shores and forests still be here? Will there be any of the spirit of my people left?"

Unfortunately, the culture of the Native Americans who were not dependant on money is almost completely overrun by the modern monetary systems. While Native American ways are still in limited practice on some reservations, the way of life that existed in the past remains primarily in spirit within some of the ideas and customs of the remaining members of the tribes that persist today. The Indians were not only forced to use and accept money but also the system of property ownership that comes with the use of money. In the case of the Native American their conversion was accomplished by law and then by enforcement of the law through war, violence and in many cases even shameful slaughter. At the time it was done with no real regard whatsoever for the way of life or welfare of the human beings themselves, who were often referred to as savages. Historically speaking, it would appear that a psychology of reckless superiority, discrimination and power are also associated with cultures that have depended on money and property rights.

By all accounts in history many Native Americans were happy and fulfilled without the need for money, which puts them at a distinct advantage over those of us whose dependency on money undermines our thinking and hinders our ability to ever feel completely fulfilled. Based on the lessons learned from our past and from cultures where people were happy without money, perhaps the there is a balance that can still be struck between what was and what exists today, for the benefit, happiness and health of the entire human race.

Chapter 4: Fiat Currencies

From the Latin for "let it be done," the word Fiat is a binding edict issued by a person in command. Fiat money is currency which derives its value from government regulation or law, or binding edict. It differs from commodity and representative money, which are based on tangibles such as a precious metal. The first known use of fiat money was recorded in China around 1000 AD.

As discussed in the previous chapters, gold and other precious metals and stones were the most significant forms of money used throughout history. However, carrying large sums of metal coin and stones can be impractical. Imagine a rich person being forced to carry their vast monetary wealth with them over great distances or for the purposes of making large purchases in distant lands. This simple problem of carrying and defending stores of bulky money, comprised of metal or stones, was one of the first reasons why paper money, called notes, came into existence. In the early days, literal paper notes in the form of letters signed with a special stamp or seal could be written by people with money that the note holder could use to redeem gold or silver from the person who wrote the note. Then the notes themselves began to be traded and used to purchase things without being immediately redeemed.

Banks also entered into the business of holding and protecting your gold, silver and precious stones for you for a fee. When you deposited your precious valuables in the bank, the bank would provide you with a receipt or a note that told how much you had at the bank and who could have access to it. The famous Knights Templar had one of the first and most elaborate networks of banks with many branches spread across Europe and into the Mediterranean that was used by people who traveled over long distances but did not want to carry money with them.

Eventually banks and other depository institutions made a practice of issuing notes that could be redeemed for specific amounts of precious metals. These notes were traded for goods and services. Similarly governments got into the business of issuing their own notes for the valuables that they stored in their treasury. Obviously if a bank or a government went out of business it would not be possible for anyone to redeem the notes (money) issued by them and in such cases it was said that the paper notes or bills "would not be worth the paper they were printed on." It was, and continues to be, important for banks and governments to be perceived as stable and honorable institutions so that people have faith that the printed paper money issued by them would really be valuable. If the credibility of any of the institutions that issued notes (money) were to be questionable then the value of the notes would also decline in value.

During its earlier history, U.S. banks issued more than 10,000 kinds of bank notes, varying in size, denomination, design and value. Many of these notes are now on display at the Museum of the City of New York. There were many problems with this system, including the shapes and sizes of notes and the instability of some banks that were poorly run. Some banks were undercapitalized and issued more notes than they could redeem in gold and silver. These reasons and many others, eventually led the U.S. Government to intervene and begin to regulate and control the money supply and the printing of money. After Congress passed, and President Wilson signed, the Federal Reserve Act in 1913, Congress established 12 District Banks to reflect the distribution of population and banking in the country. These banks are private banks and to this day much controversy exists over their inner workings and ownership. Then in 1933 President Franklin Roosevelt took the U.S. off the gold standard and the nation was explicitly using fiat money for the first time. Neither the U.S. Government nor U.S. banks were forced to redeem money for gold or silver. Instead the use and value of the U.S. Dollar was implemented by Fiat or decree of law. In 1935, the U.S. Congress created the Federal Open Market Committee, to be the Fed's monetary policy arm in order to create a formal authority to ensure that monetary policies would be carried out responsibly.

There was a real need to take the country off the gold standard when you consider that there was and is still simply not enough gold to go around, in either the vaults of banks nor in the treasuries of the government. In spite of the fact that the U.S. dollar was suddenly no longer able to be redeemed for gold or silver, the U.S. dollar continues to retain significant value for purchasing goods and services.

There are numerous risks and mistakes that can be made in the implementation and use of fiat currencies for any country. It must have been very difficult and troubling to change the entire monetary system in the United States and yet the country did not disintegrate as a result of these monumental changes. However, I believe that it would be unreasonable to expect that any country on Earth could get it all right on the first try, and to expect that there would not be an ongoing evolutionary process of the money system. As successful as it has been for the U.S. to make use of fiat currency there are still many imperfections and loopholes in the existing system and many improvements that can be made to the system, in particular the major potential advancements that are the subject of this book.

The act of taking the U.S. off of the gold standard and having the currency retain useful value as it has until now has been a great example that proves that money in of itself is an abstraction whose value and usefulness is determined by agreements between people. In the case of the U.S. dollar the agreements, backed by the force of law, law enforcement officers and the U.S. military, have been a compelling reason for people to treat the dollar as valuable and use it as a medium of trade. I imagine that there was a compelling argument at the time of the transition of the money system that any country who did not accept the U.S. fiat money as valuable would have to contend with the U.S. military. I think that this is a profound and valid argument that is even more applicable in this day and age.

The act of taking the country off of the gold standard required many fascinating mechanisms upheld by law (agreement of force), such as the ability of banks to seemingly create money as needed by using a system of credit and debt. In fact the fine details about our money system are generally unknown or misunderstood by the average U.S. citizen. Some of this confusion has led to the development and use of systems of law such as the U.S. Uniform Commercial Codes.

Every year since its creation the U.S. Federal Reserve (or "the Fed") publishes a great deal of information that can be obtained free of charge from their website. This can enlighten U.S. citizens and the people of the world on the intricacies of the U.S. monetary and banking systems. Reading these publications can help one to unravel astonishing facts that have practical use in everyday life. It is amazing that some information that is critical of the commercial banks themselves and our entire monetary system can be freely obtained directly from the U.S. Federal Reserve.

A careful examination and study of this information

and associated court cases can help ordinary home owners truly understand their rights, by law, with regards to their mortgages and other loans, and repayment of credit that was extended. The relationship and use of cash accounts verses credit accounts to make purchases in the U.S. using credit extended by U.S. banks is a complex subject in itself. Most people have no idea that U.S. banks keep two sets of books; one for cash accounting and one for the credit accounting. Although the subject of credit versus cash accounts as used by banks is beyond the scope of this book I encourage all U.S. citizens to attempt, for their own good, to better understand the facility of the issuance of credit in the way it is actually implemented in our laws rather than how it is usually practiced and abused. The U.S. credit system is, at core, the temporary creation of money and the expansion and contraction of the cash supply in the U.S. economy. For those who unravel the mysteries of the credit and lending system there may be substantial benefits.

For the purposes of our subject it is important to realize that the paper money issued by most governments in the world can no longer be redeemed for any treasure or precious metal. You may have the ability to use paper money to buy gold or other treasures for as long as people consider the money valuable, but the issuers of the money, banks and/or governments rarely redeem money for hard tangible assets themselves. Most of the people in the world are already dependant on fiat money (or currency) in one way or another for their everyday existence and therefore most people rely heavily on the governments to regulate the creation and use of fiat money.

In our society it is the governments of the world that establish the rules of money and economics. Fiat money is created by governments either directly or indirectly and so it stands to reason that force of law impacts the value of money. I like to restate this important idea from the last chapter because it is a key concept throughout this book. The idea is that, because laws represent the agreements, imposed by force on people by government, governments typically exert the greatest influence and control over the value of money, and governments are routinely in charge of, or mandate banks, in creating and regulating the physical manifestation and use of money, including coins, bills, credit and their electronic counterparts.

Today digital and virtual currencies are being created and used by people all around the world for a variety of reasons. However, at least for the time being, use of these virtual currencies does not appear to threaten any government because they typically must be converted back into the currency of some country at some time in order for the underlying value to be redeemed. Unless current use of virtual currencies changes, it is unlikely that governments like the United States will interfere with the creation of these new currencies. For the time being virtual currencies appear to be nothing more than a new means of transmission and storage of already established currencies of the world governments. The value of virtual currencies also varies adding yet another instrument that can be used for speculation and gambling otherwise referred to as "investing" or "trading".

As of the writing of this book we have tried a variety of experiments in the money system of the United States, including using a "gold standard", creating the edifice of the U.S. Federal Reserve, fixing currency rates, then allowing the currency rates to float and simply printing money as needed by allowing more money to be accessed by the government through credit (i.e. allowing for the expansion of the national debt). Since 2008, we have seen the default of some state and local governments in the USA, such as in Detroit, and in the world we've seen entire countries, such as Greece and Cyprus, fail economically and their citizens' way of life effected. Our present day implementations and use of money appear to leave us vulnerable to uncertain and devastating changes in the valuations of our currencies and the purchasing power of our money. Our monetary systems appear to leave entire governments vulnerable to collapse and their citizens subject to rapid devaluations of their property and loss of lifestyles. And while there have been many social programs that have improved the general welfare of people overall, the sustainability and viability of these programs is also threatened by the monetary, economic and tax systems of the world.

Today there are many groups which acknowledge that there is something missing from our current monetary and economic systems. The most popular ways of thinking about economics and money policies are usually expressed as agenda's by political parties or other social groups. Some of the solutions being argued for in capitalist economies are either calls to go back to the gold standard, or calls to eliminate institutions such as the U.S. Federal Reserve. There are also more abstract concepts which sound appealing in theory but for which there are no practical road maps for implementation, such as the noteworthy idea of the "resource based economy". All of the ideas about economic and monetary policies have their champions; however, the subject of this book is to introduce a new way that I believe will simultaneously satisfy each of the major camps in politics, economics and the monetary administration of today. For instance I am in favor of the idea of creating a resource based economy in principal. However, until now there has been no practical road map offered by anyone that will enable us to peacefully begin to transition to such an idealist ways of life. In my opinion, the solutions that I propose provide the practical means by which we can move towards the implementation of such ideal societies and economies with little or no resistance from any of the major political, business or individual interests that currently exist globally.

Whatever system is to become the next phase of our way of life on earth the ideas in this book will help ease us through those transitions and into the future, be it a resource based economy or any other form.

Part 2
So What is the Problem

According to Albert Einstein the problems facing us today cannot be solved using the same thinking that created the problems in the first place. So, before we explore the solutions presented in this book, let's look at some of the most popular arguments in economics, from the perspective of the common man in the street. Let us expose some of problems in respect to what is currently being advocated based on our historical experiences. I am not attempting to create an exhaustive list of all of the popular modes of thinking about the U.S. economy and its monetary policies today, but to simply examine a handful of ideas which I believe most U.S. citizens may have heard before or been lead to believe themselves.

Chapter 6: Where We've Been & Where We Are
The Gold Standard

Arguments in favor of using the gold standard for monetary value is often associated with Conservative, Republican and Libertarian political groups. These people claim that the government went in the wrong direction when it abandoned the gold standard and that the U.S. Government should return to money whose value is associated with gold. Examining our previous use of the gold standard, let's look at some of the biggest problems, in my opinion, with basing the value of our currency on a commodity such as gold.

When the government ran out of gold it took the gold needed from it from its citizens by force of law in exchange for new currency in 1934. The U.S. Gold Reserve Act outlawed most private possession of gold, forcing individuals to sell it to the U.S. Treasury, after which it was stored in the United States Bullion Depository at Fort Knox and other locations. People who collect and trade gold coins today in the United States in order to protect themselves against devaluation of the dollar seem to completely forget this chapter in U.S. history where people were simply compelled to turn their gold over to the government in exchange for paper. Additionally, because of the concept that there is simply not enough gold to go around for the world's current population to use as a money supply it introduces a practical problem with redemption for gold that can never be fixed.

The only practical way of returning to a gold standard today would be for a country such as the U.S. to decree by law that the value of one U.S. dollar is equal in value to a specific amount of gold. Requiring the government and banks to store and redeem gold is not an option because the supply of gold in the world is limited and no government is in possession of enough gold to even make redemption and storage of gold a viable option. Thus, the re-implementation of the gold standard in relation to money would essentially boil down to imposing a specific price range for gold or imposing price controls in relation to a specific currency. I am not opposed to using price controls to help sustain the value of a currency. In fact I can even see some merit in locking the value of money into a rare commodity such as gold because it may also help to curb inflation. However, there is an obvious problem with permanently fixing the rate(s) of exchange on any specific commodity and that involves the necessity of the valuation to change according to costs associating with procuring the commodity. In other words, what happens if gold suddenly becomes too costly to mine given the established rates of exchange? Or what happens if mining gold from asteroids yields so much gold that gold is no longer rare? In these cases it is conceivable that we may need to perform revaluations in the future that would introduce an unnecessary complexity. All that we really care about is the relationship between our currency and that of others, not our currency in relation to any particular commodity.

Using gold as the permanent standard will therefore not solve the problem in the stability of the value of money because the value of gold itself can fluctuate. Besides which, who can really say that gold is valuable at all, particularly in times of natural disasters and emergencies? Since gold itself is not necessary to sustain life, then what happens to our currency as the price of gold fluctuates? Why bother to introduce this kind of avoidable scenario?

Basing the value of any money on any naturally occurring element may arbitrarily cause an imbalance between countries that happen to have large reserves and those countries that do not. Countries that have more gold than others may gain an advantage and those that do not have an abundant supply may be at a disadvantage without any justification. Gold was already the cause of many wars of the past. This is an enduring problem that could lead to wars again, in the same way as oil is thought to be a motivator of the major wars of our times.

Valuing a currency based on gold or on any object requires a decree of law by the government and physical enforcement of the rule. Such a system would be redundant because the government can simply decree the value of money at any time by force without having to associate it directly with gold. On January 6, 1942, President Franklin D. Roosevelt announced some ambitious production goals to support the war effort. As a result, all of the country's economic sectors were placed under increased government control. While economists usually oppose price controls, it was a state of emergency. Isn't it always the case that an emergency requires extreme actions? For reasons I will make clear later in this book I contend that we are actually in a state of economic emergency today. On August 15, 1971, President Richard M. Nixon announced that the United States was abandoning the gold standard and imposed a 90-day freeze on prices and wages, which was the beginning of the end of the Bretton Woods system of international currency management established after World War II.

The point is that, if prices can be controlled by decree of law and international currency exchange rate agreements, such as Bretton Woods, then what is the point or the need to associate any money with any commodity other than in times of emergency or as a measure to defeat inflation? The value of money can be established by law. Again, the mere consideration of the gold standard only reinforces the concept developed again and again in this book that money is only as valuable as people agree it is, either by force of law or by some other convention, belief or agreement.

Keynesian Economics

In the U.S. arguments around the value of money remaining unchanged in light of large deficit spending or large increases in money supplies has often been associated with liberal and democratic schools of thought. Large government deficit spending and subsequent higher rates of income tax are typically thought by many to accompany the use of Keynesian economic policies.

Keynesian economics is based on the philosophies of British economist John Maynard Keynes who, during the 1930's, attempted to deal with the effects of the Great Depression. Keynes advocated increased government expenditures and lower taxes to stimulate demand and pull the global economy out of the Depression. Keynes advocated government intervention with the economy in order to stimulate growth during economic crises.

I like the concepts of Keynesian economics because it forces those who consider it to also consider the abstraction of the use of money itself. There is no economy without money being spent and conversely without people to spend money there is no economy at all. If there is no money changing hands then who is to say that money has any value at all? Again, the only utility of money is that others will accept money in exchange for goods and services. If nobody is exchanging any money then what good is it?

If you want to stimulate the economy, then you have to put money in the hands of people so that they can spend it! It is hard to argue with the effectiveness of this philosophy and it is also hard to argue that increased government spending that creates jobs will not help to stimulate positive growth in the economy.

The value of money can be established and regulated by law, and enforced by government. It has been so throughout history.

The fundamental problems with the implementation of Keynesian economic policies in the United States and in other countries is not with the obvious fact that government spending can help create jobs and improve the economy, but that, due to the constructs of present day money systems, governments are often required to spend more than they are taking in through taxes in order to create jobs or even to perform the basic tasks that people have come to expect from them. According to our current implementation of money systems, this excessive spending by government requires that the money be paid back, in most cases with interest.

This penalty of the need for tax payers to pay money back with interest that is borrowed by the government creates a genuine problem with the effectiveness of government and with the use of Keynesian economic policies that require large government expenditure. Thus, although government spending obviously can help stimulate an economy and repair it, the costs associated with creating government programs in taxes and repayment of deficits act as a deterrent from full blown Keynesian spending. It has also led people to criticize Keynesian economics and even label it as a communist invention that eventually forces the re-distribution of wealth through higher tax burdens.

Understand this, the entire problem of government deficits and the need to foot the bill with interest is illogical in the first place. In order to have an economy, you have to have people and the people have to have money in their hands to spend. Thus, for a vibrant economy money must come from somewhere. If the government were to simply hand it out without the need for anyone to repay the money then is there any reason to say the same money is any less valuable? In reality, there is no reason other than set ideas in our minds. What keeps us from fashioning the money system as we need it rather than accept it as is? Wrong thinking, false ideas and fear hold us back just as they do in many aspects of human life.

Does any reader honestly believe that there are any governments that actually want to see the U.S. dollar become worthless? Why would any society want that? Even some of the greatest enemies of the U.S. still rely on the U.S. dollar as a means of trade. Certainly no person who holds U.S. dollars in their account wants the value to go down even if they disagree with the policies of the U.S. Government. And with what would we replace the U.S. dollar? One must also note that the same challenges the U.S. faces as a result of the way it creates its money is reflected in most other countries. So if the U.S. experiences inflation, then other globally integrated countries are also usually experiencing similar rates of inflation. Inflation is a psychological effect of the use of money and of the idea of a return on investment and inflation can be regulated and overcome by force of law.

In subsequent chapters I discuss inflation and ways to cope with it in more detail. For the time being consider that inflation is simply a psychological effect of the use of money and the collective desire of mankind to receive more money for less work, i.e. interest earned off the work of others. Inflation will always exist in a variety of manifestations and it can only be controlled through force of law and related actions, including revaluation laws and/or price controls.

Thus the utilization of Keynesian economic policies has and continues to be one of the things that will be better able help our economies to evolve to the next state of existence. The use of Keynesian policies forces us to confront the issues around government deficit spending and its effect on taxes and the value of currency. Use of Keynesian economic policies is helping us to dispel the phantom problems caused largely by our failure to realize what creates the value of money itself. The value of money is based on perception, agreements and the desire for the money to succeed. All of these things, perception, agreements and desire, can all be regulated by the laws of government. If it were not so then how would it be possible for the U.S. dollar to still retain its power while trillions of dollars in record government deficit spending has caused the money supply to grow?

It is the sheer will and collective desire of the people of the world that the U.S. dollar retain its value and so it does, no matter how much is printed. Now what needs to occur is an overhaul of the methods by which the government prints money, who it gives it to and how the money supply is increased and decreased based on the size of the global population. We can no longer live in the fantasy world of false belief that the global population can increase without boundaries as rapidly as it does, but that, at the same time, no more money needs to be available. In order for the economy to exist, you must have two things, people and sufficient money for each person to spend. I argue that the current supply of fiat money in today's world is simply not enough to sustain the basic standards of living which many people have come to expect and which all needy people aspire to. Just like the problem of the gold running out of U.S. Treasury in the 1930's we have a similar problem of lack of currency itself. The method of lending money into existence that must be repaid is proven to be inadequate to increase and equitably distribute the supply of money. Other than government deficit spending, lending money into existence is not even available as an option for poor people and will do nothing to end poverty.

The way in which fiat currency has been created in the U.S. for the last 60 years has now led us to experience and realize that something is missing from the current monetary system.

Occupy Wall Street

The movement known as Occupy Wall Street occurred in the wake of the global financial crisis of 2008. Occupy Wall Street (OWS) began on September 17, 2011, in Zuccotti Park, located in New York City's Wall Street financial district, receiving global attention and spawning the Occupy movement against social and economic inequality worldwide.

The Occupy protesters' slogan "We are the 99%" refers to the protester's perceptions of, and attitudes regarding, income disparity in the U.S. (and globally) and economic inequality in general, which have been the main issues addressed by OWS. OWS's goals include a reduction in the influence of corporations on politics, a more balanced distribution of wealth, more and better jobs, bank reform (especially to curtail speculative trading by banks), forgiveness of student loan debt or other relief for indebted students, and alleviation of property foreclosures.

It is unclear into what political classifications those who participated in OWS might fall, what the implementation of their goals might look like, or how they might impact taxation or tax rates. Some called them anti-capitalists, while others said that they stood for strengthening of capitalist principals like accountability.

For mainstream U.S. society I believe that the goals and arguments of the movement as a whole were unclear or unrealized other than to simply complain about the plight of the poor in the world and in the U.S., the influence of big business with government, and the practices of big business and financially wealthy people that exacerbate economic inequality in the world.

For many people observing the protests from the outside there seemed to be an undertone of a sense of entitlement by the protestors, many of whom occupied abandon foreclosed homes saying things such as, "We all deserve homes, it's our right as human beings." These ideas sounded too much like, "I deserve something for nothing, and you (successful business owners and tax payers) must give it to me for free."

I do believe that these protests did and still do capture at least one sentiment that resonates within all American's and that has not yet been adequately articulated with regards to a major failure of our current government and economic system, and those of the entire world. The sentiment is essentially, "why can't we get this right for everyone?" It leads us to ask questions like, "Who is really running things here? And why can't we solve the problems of poverty and the economic problems to which each of us have become subjected to by our own governments and systems over which we are lead to believe we have some control?"

Chapter 7: What People Are Trying To Say

For God And Country

If you are born a king and I am born as a serf living on your land, then why is it my duty to live my life in servitude to you just because you have the title of king? Why were you born with land and money at your disposal and I have none? Why don't you simply give me some of your wealth so we can become more equal?

One of the traditional answers to these questions is to tell people to take up the issue with God. As if the present day economies and governments and their random nature are something that God put into place rather than us. The idea of the randomness of our fate as being born into financial opportunity or financial poverty is as silly as blaming God for the meltdown of a nuclear reactor that we built or those who suffered under the institution of slavery that we implemented. Blaming God is a convenient way for people fail to take responsibility for their own role in the continuance of the problems.

No matter what your spiritual inclinations it is generally accepted that we have the gift of free will to do we like and treat people however we choose. It was not God who implemented our current global system of property rights and ownership with its random selection process for gracing some at birth while condemning others. It was not God who insisted on having kings and queens to rule over us. In the old testament of the Bible it was the people themselves who begged for the installation of a king against the advice of the spiritual leaders of the day. Some would say that it is within our human nature to appoint people to rule over us. However, I would say that it has been a failed experiment, from which human nature is evolving, and which will eventually be rejected. If you were to examine people in their most natural condition you might find that the appointment of leaders was achieved by concession, necessity or force rather than by nature.

As an example consider Native Americans, as well as many other cultures throughout history, who have lived happily enjoying spiritually rich and healthy lives by sharing everything that was available without our present day system of property ownership and segregation. There are many groups throughout history that did govern by individual representation and group consensus without the need for kings or queens. One could argue very easily that it is our practice of property ownership and rights and our practices of appointing others to govern over us that is actually the less sophisticated way of life. It follows that many aspects of the system continue to fail us in its current manifestation.

As a Christian I have and continue to make an in-depth study of the writings of the apostles as well as many other religions and spiritual texts and beliefs. From my research it would appear that the underlying ideas about financial wealth are similar across the vast majority of spiritual and religious texts and teachings. If I were to summarize the most important message underlying each of the major religions it would be that we need to make our life a mission to overcome our own selfishness for the good of humanity, because we are all connected. When it comes to the religious and spiritual aspects of money spoken about in various texts, there is the idea that true wealth and happiness is not derived from the ownership of money or property and that those who are financially wealthy have a responsibility to assist and treat fairly those who are not.

So the problem with blaming God is that God places the issue back on you and I, and our implementation of our own economy, government, money and lives.

Christian scriptures are quite clear when it comes to financial wealth; "love of money is the root of all evil" and "if you want to follow me rid yourself of your selfish ways" and "give to Caesar what is Cesar's", "none had want for anything because we all shared it," and of course, "If you want to follow me give everything that you own to the poor."

So is it the selfishness of the king or the wealthy people for wanting to remain rich that is the cause of my suffering? Well perhaps that is a major component that drives the current financial imbalances that plague our lives today. In the U.S. we complicate matters even more as we are supposed to live under an elected government with no hereditary class of nobility. We are supposed to have a system of government, according to our constitution, where we are all equal. There are supposed to be no kings in our society. The problem is that not all equal people are born into equal circumstances. Yes most of us are equal in the sense that we have two arms and legs and hands and we are, at least in theory entitled to the same protections under the law, however, those born into wealthy families will generally have many more opportunities in their lives than those that are born into poor families and so it is impossible for everyone to have an equal chance in life.

Hence, the argument that we all feel in the pit of our stomach can be summarized as follows: "If our government truly reflects the will of the people, then why do it and its laws so unequally favor the rich? If the rich are entitled to protection for their property, then what are the rest of the people entitled to receive when they have none?" Those who are financially disadvantaged might be driven to action by questions like, "Why is it that just because one person is born into wealth that I must become a slave to money for the rest of my life and serve those who are rich? Why can't I just live off the land that God made for us all?" This concept of living off the land and sharing was the same sentiment spoken about by the Native Americans when they were overtaken by our Eurocentric society.

This last question really cuts right to the root of the problem that we all feel within us but that has never really been articulated in the way I will attempt to put into words now.

The Problems With Property & Government

Because of the existence of governments, there are very few places on earth where you can live freely on a piece of land that has enough resources on it to survive. Yes there are some reservations for indigenous people that you can live on. However, it is unlikely that you will be able to use the majority of any of the modern conveniences on these lands even if you qualify by ethnicity to live there.

A primary function of the modern European style of government is to divide property amongst people and regulate the usage of it. The primary reason why the Native Americans were so ferociously eradicated into virtual extinction is because their way of life did not include the segregation of property between people, but somehow managed to harmoniously allow for the sharing and use of property by all. The concept of ownership was radically different and virtually non-existent in a great deal of the Native American culture.

In addition, the Native American's had entire governments and agreements that were represented by images instead of written words and where each person was able to speak for themselves and represent themselves in the meetings of the tribes. Decisions of the tribe were based on consensus that was arrived at by the direct participation of each member of the tribe rather than by proxy where intentions can be misrepresented. This Native American method of self government and of non-existent property rights, no matter how superior in implementation, peacekeeping, spirituality or in results, was a direct threat to the arguably less sophisticated method of government of the Europeans.

The European (now "Western") methods of government inspires selfishness, mandates inequality, division of property and caters to an artificial and stifling idea of ownership of things rather thatn use and sharing of things while we are alive. These ideas have repeatedly been the basis for war.

The problem is that, in practice, most modern governments of the world exist to do only a few fundamental things. Protect lives, protect property and govern the use of property. If you are born into a life where you own no property then you have access to less property (and resources) to make use of, and there will exist reduced capacity in the potential of your life. This is the direct result of the current design and implementation of our modern style of government.

In essence we are born into lives that are structured for us by our governments whether we like it or not. And one of the as yet unresolved consequences of the nature of our current human world is that the vast majority of people, who ARE NOT born into wealth or property ownership, have already had something arbitrarily taken away from them at birth, and that is the use of the land and all that is on it. In the initial formation of the United States only white, male land owners could vote until 1850. While things have changed since that time in terms of voting, other issues around property and ownership have not changed and the original foundational thinking persists.

Even to this day the use of the land and all that resides on it is reserved for the wealthy as enforced by government. This is true whether someone lives in a so called capitalist country, a statist country, a socialist country or even in a communist country. While it is a fact that Native American tribes did also fight against each other for resources, they were not predisposed to actually believe that they owned the property for which they fought and they did not have kings and queens or governments that could easily be corrupted by individual greed for accumulation of financial wealth, but leaders who were motivated by consensus. In contrast the problems of inequality that we experience are built, by design, into our governments. And most people are so busy just trying to make ends meet that they have no time to participate in their own government. Fortunately these are mechanisms that can be altered for the greater good without making substantial changes at all. I believe that in order to set things right, what needs to occur is that some simple compensation be given to all people to make up for what has been taken from them. What I propose is not to take from the rich to give to the poor or to demand that everyone be financially equalized, but something slightly different that simply leverages the powers of the same governments that create the problem in the first place, to solve the problems and assist the poor without taking from anyone.

Property is something that we cannot take with us

when we die. Ironically people think of a piece of property as something that they actually do own, when in reality all land, and that which sits on it, is owned by the government according to our existing conventions. It can be taken away from anyone without any due process at any time by the government. Even in the United States, where we are taught that people can get rich and own anything, if someone fails to pay tax the government can simply seize assets at any time. The government also routinely regulates the activities that take place on all properties. There are many legal cases which illustrate how the U.S. Government, which is supposed to be a hallmark of due legal process, routinely seizes property from people without notice or good cause. This happens for a variety of reasons, including suspicion of criminal activity alone, even where there is no evidence and where no trail has begun. Similar unfair government mechanisms exist in one form or another in most of the countries of the world.

At best we rent property from the government but we do not really own it, nor can we take it to the grave. Although it is not necessary to give up any perceived ideas or any of the current mechanisms surrounding ownership of anything in order to utilize the ideas presented in this book, I do believe as a practicing Consciousness Coach that it is healthy for people to relieve themselves of the burdens that are associated with the false ideas of property ownership. I have seen that the expectations surrounding ownership of property can lead to mental and physical stress and ultimately disease.

The fact that we are indoctrinated into a system of beliefs about property ownership does not make the current system right or wrong, but rather something that can be improved. Do I advocate that we do away with property rights? No. We are far to dependant on these systems of ownership and money for us to change our system to do away with property rights. I do not believe that it is entirely necessary either, but rather to modify our governments and monetary policies in order to improve upon the current systems for the good of everyone. I do believe that we are in a point in our history were we can make dramatic changes through enacting some simple laws and agreements in one or more of our governments that will enable a revolutionary change in the overall welfare of both the rich and the poor without taking anything away from anyone. In later chapters I even offer potential solutions that do not require action by any government in order to effect change. These can be implemented by people around the world who believe in the ideas of this book.

The problems of inequality exist in relation to the fact that some people are born into wealth, or otherwise work to obtain it, and others are not born into wealth and are unable to attain it for whatever reason. These same problems manifest themselves in the macrocosm of global economies and between counties. Consider the case where one country has large gold or oil reserves when compared to other countries. For example, the standard of living in Saudi Arabia, Kuwait and Norway is very high as its citizens benefit from the money that comes from their oilfields. In contrast there is a lower quality of the life of citizens of other countries who have no deposits of gold, oil or other valuables, or where the wealth of such minerals remains unlocked or unequally distributed throughout the citizenry. The problems between those born into wealthy families or wealthy countries are not to be blamed on anyone or any government in particular but they are problems that can be solved in our modern society without blaming or taking anything away from anyone.

If it is truly the goal of a caring society for all people to be able to live a happy life with as much potential for their lives sharing in modern conveniences, then there is an inherent problem with the current manifestation of our systems of government and economies. The good news is that there are several painless ways to help restore opportunity to those who have little while still allowing the wealthy to enjoy the fruits of their good fortune and work.

Another Choice

In this book I will share another choice in economic and monetary policy that I believe will satisfy the needs of those who want to eliminate income tax and replace the social welfare systems altogether. At the same time, it dramatically improves availability of resources to government to lift the overall welfare, quality of life, happiness, education and medical care for everyone in the world.

This revolutionary economic and monetary system can be easily implemented today, with or without the help of government, and it requires no changes to any of our conventional uses of property. In fact, the fundamental ideas are already being successfully implemented in various governments of the world, either directly or indirectly, or even out of necessity. If one or more governments, or the people within them, were to participate in this new economy through the passage and enforcement of a handful of laws or by taking the actions described in this book, then there would be no need for income taxes and government spending could be allowed to be increased as required in order to deliver quality services to their citizens. Simple global treaties could be established that would permanently eliminate economic disasters between nations.

In the United States we have become a nation of people that are obsessed in finding and allocating blame to others for any problems that we experience. At the first sign of any trouble we can't wait to force someone to resign, or throw someone in jail and take away everything they have. This is not a healthy way to live. Without the ability to forgive and move on nobody can grow. The wealthy are not evil, nor are the poor. The governments are not necessarily at fault either as the current problem of inequality has existed for ages and is the result of old thinking that can be remedied.

There is a solution to the problems with which we are faced. **The first step to the solution is to find an equitable way to compensate those who are not wealthy for the use (forced usurpation) of property that has been arbitrarily removed from them by birth or through mismanagement for the benefit of those who are born wealthy or become wealthy during their lives.**

Chapter 8: The Problem To Be Solved

There is imbalance between the natural and intellectual resources of countries. Some countries with access to superior natural resources are able to provide more for their citizens. Similarly there exists imbalance between people who are born at the same time where some are born into wealth and others not born into wealth. Given our awareness of these random imbalances and given the fact that governments operate by our design there must be something that we can do to compensate.

If you were to poll the majority of people in the world today about their greatest problems or the greatest source of suffering in their lives, I believe that the most common answers would include adequate housing, food, medical care, education, free time, entertainment and access to opportunity. These are the basic problems that face people not born into wealth. The lack of any of these things creates circumstances conducive to a lifetime of unfulfilling servitude. Lack of any one of these things can also lead to the commission of crimes and deviant behavior that negatively impacts everyone. Helping people to overcome these inequalities to simply sustain a comfortable and fulfilling life is something that can be achieved today.

It is said that life often imitates art. George Orwell's novel (and later movie) "1984" describes a futuristic, totalitarian regime in which people are watched and ruled by their government through a shadowy figure known as Big Brother. When I was a child I was frequently told by "conspiracy theorist" that someday the government would be able to know exactly where you are at all times and would be able to listen in on your conversations and watch you through real time video feeds coming from common everyday places and appliances. I was told that anyone could potentially be abducted without due process of law, held and even tortured by the authorities. With the pervasive use of mobile phones, personal computers and the internet, and using terrorism as an excuse, virtually all of what was formerly referred to as conspiracy theory has become reality. These practices are now a matter of public knowledge because of people like:

- Edward Snowden who exposed the nature of the work he did for the U.S. Government

- Maher Arar the Canadian citizen who sued the U.S. after being abducted by the U.S. government, without due process, and sent to Syria for months of torture, thereby revealing these secret torture locations used by the U.S. and its allies.

There was a time when we said that we would rather let one hundred criminals go free than convict one innocent man. Today it appears that we don't care how many innocent people go to jail or are tortured for the sake of our "security".

It is painfully clear how the systems of government can be used and abused by manipulation of public opinion and, more importantly, public fear and our own human nature. The good news is that there is also potential for the government to be used as a means to implement positive and constructive practices that benefit all the people of the world. We will never be able to completely rid ourselves of the undesirable components of human nature by ourselves but we can and should always strive to become better. Just as governments can do great harm because they are comprised of people, they can also do great good.

One of my favorite science fiction movies and television shows is the Star Trek series. Much of the science and technology described in the Star Trek series is today becoming reality. What would really be amazing is if we could somehow achieve the described economic accomplishments of the elimination of poverty and individual pursuit of accomplishment and fulfillment. In the future shown by Star Trek it appears there is no poverty amongst the inhabitants of Earth and the members of Star Fleet and people seem to be happy and healthy and everyone appears to have access to adequate medical care. It also appears that somehow people are free to explore their fullest potential by pursuing careers in which they are truly interested rather than being forced to work at jobs that they don't want in order to simply "exist" rather than live. Clearly money still exists in the Star Trek future as does greed, wealth, reckless ambition and other undesirable side effects of the use of money and our human nature. However, there does not seem to be any immediacy for anyone to do anything in particular in order to provide for their day to day survival other than to pursue as work things that are of interest to them.

I believe that we are at an evolutionary point in our history where it is possible to realistically achieve this state of affairs throughout the world, and thereby enable people to unlock their own greatest potential. For some people their greatest potential may be to sit on a sofa and eat potato chips for the rest of their lives. Poverty or not, there will always be some people who choose to do nothing in their lives of any significance, and who are we to say that they are wrong? Even these people can make a valuable contribution to the velocity of money and to a healthy economy because of their capacity to be consumers.

Enormous strides have seemingly been made in improving the lives of many people, mostly in advanced nations. However, this cloaks what is reality for the vast majority of humanity around the world. No matter what system of government they live under, whether a monarchy, democracy, republic, statist, communist or socialist regime, the primary focus for the majority of people remains basic survival. Their lives have not changed substantially from the serfs living under the nobility of previous centuries. Even in the United States there are many such people. The disparity between rich and poor is growing, and fast.

A common misconception is that poor people are somehow lazy, uneducated and less deserving, hence the outcome of their lives. This view disallows the interconnection between us all, and the impact everyone feels or will feel in the future for the failure to consider the lives of so many others. We need to act to solve the issues of education and poverty because they simply aren't someone else's responsibility, nor will they solve themselves.

For those of us who find ourselves in the fortunate position of living ostensibly better lives, consider that our circumstances may have changed but our basic human worries still have not. It is true that we live in better homes and we use cars and airplanes instead of horses and we have phones instead of messengers; we are all better connected to each other through television, radio and the internet and we have advanced medical capabilities. However, it is also true that there are still those who have and those who have not. Thus, as we see with many homeless people, a simple set of circumstances can change a person's status from a "have" to a "have not" in a short space of time and for a variety of reasons.

In our world there are still kings and lords but today we call them elected officials, presidents and judges.   Governments are still swayed and controlled by powerful individuals and their business interests; politicians often behave just like celebrities and salespeople with questionable integrity.   Modern justice systems and law enforcement are still corrupt and operate above the law, largely unaccountable to anyone. For every disease or medical condition that we've overcome more have sprung up. In spite of all our modern science, inventions and new age spirituality, the nature of the lives and concerns of people throughout recorded history have not changed very much at all.

Let's take a brief look at what life looks like today for people in the U.S. and any other developed nation. For a handful of wealthy people the world is their playground, whether they worked for the money, inherited it or were born into it. For the rest of the middle class and the poor the way in which we live most of our lives can be compared to a day at the amusement park.   When wealthy people go to the amusement park then can afford to eat all of the food, play all of the games, shop at the stores and pay to skip to the front of the lines. Some in the middle class wait in lines for the rides and eat some of the food and they might even be able to buy a souvenir if they manage their money. The poor sleep in the forest on the other side of town from the park. They've seen the park on T.V. and on reality shows and they are lucky if they can gain entry to the amusement park at all. The poor walk through the souvenir shop, watch the rich and middle class ride all the rides and smell the food, but the poor might not have enough money to buy tickets to ride on any of the rides or even eat any of the food. They may drink from the water fountains or pick up discarded scraps when they are hungry or thirsty. Sometimes a wealthy person offers to pay the way for a poor person to experience the park for a day. And sometimes someone from the middle class shares some of their food with the poor. If the poor are really lucky they can get a job working at the amusement park, but the jobs are too few and most of the poor are unqualified for the work.

In this day and age there is at least one area where we can make some immediate and positive progress and this is in the area of truly bringing provisions to those who currently have not, without taking from those who have. That is what this book is about.

Current economic policies inspire discrimination and selfishness throughout the world, keep us from realizing our mutual needs for one another, and stifle our ability to grow as a species. Current economic systems inspire attitudes such as "I have mine, you go get yours." Governments are forced to pick the pockets of people who have worked hard for themselves in order to give to others, thus creating resentment towards the poor. We have created the conditions for the attitude that the poor are of less value than the rich. We've misplaced the very essence of what wealth is and I believe that we stand to lose our entire species if we do not eventually correct this problem. Some say money is the problem; I say our use of money can be the best cure. I believe that when money is made to function properly it can be a catalyst that unlocks the full potential of every human being, making it possible for us all to do and study what truly interests us during our lifetimes, and it can change the present course of humanity.

Deep within us we all believe that there is something missing from our present economic systems that relegate some to extreme poverty and others in extreme wealth, and most to lives that amount to nothing more than "making ends meet". Isn't there more to life, or is there only more for those who have more money? The truth is that it is only by our mutual current design that people are made to falsely believe that the only solutions revolve around taking money from the rich to give to others. There are other far more efficient and equitable measures for us to correct the problem of poverty. There is a way to compensate for the use of property that has been taken from people by the construct of government. There is a simple way to provide each and every person with access to the necessities that enable them to live lives that are truly more fulfilling.

This book provides the foundation for a simple economic mechanism that can be implemented in a practical manner in our lifetimes and that can liberate us all from having to live a life where people are forced to work at jobs and pursue careers and lifestyles in which they are unhappy. Am I talking about the end of fast food restaurants? No what I'm talking about is a society where those who work in such jobs can do so because they like the work and they can hold such jobs with respect and with financial security that they do not have now. This does not change the business model, the current responsibilities, or benefits to those who own the businesses. Using the methods that I provide in this book there is no need to even change the minimum wage.

Chapter 9: Human Thinking About Money

As a certified Consciousness Coach one of the most amazing life improving truths that I am privileged to be able to share with people is that, while they may not have control over all of the external circumstances of their life, they do posses great control over how they react and behave. It is within our own ability to change our behavior for the better in order to achieve goals in spite of our prior thinking, beliefs and feelings. It is this that makes us powerful beings. We don't need to be subjugated in our lives by false thinking and feelings that interfere with our own abilities. Many people live their lives crippled by their own thinking and feelings. Many people are unaware that they have a choice and are able to take constructive courses of action even if this new behavior conflicts with their old thinking and feelings.

Our true power as human beings lies in the fact that we can engineer our own behavior. Our individual personalities do not represent who we actually are or what we are truly capable of but our personalities are the result of a set of ideas about ourselves that we chose to believe. Thus if we chose to believe, or as Christians say, "have faith", in some new concept of what we can be, then we can transform. Although it is not without difficulty we can consciously design our behavior for the better. Similarly the laws created by our government represent the personality of each government. Our laws represent the ideas that we chose to believe in for a variety of reasons. Sometimes our laws, just like our individual beliefs, do not inspire action and behavior that we know will lead to favorable results. Both humans and governments are fallible and are in a constant state of evolution. Since our governments, laws and economies are representative of our collective beliefs then they can be modified as we can modify our individual beliefs and personalities. Sometimes laws enacted by government, which have a great deal of influence on our behaviors, can be changed more easily than our own false beliefs can be changed.

Our modern economies function within a framework of laws and in theory our laws can be changed in order to accommodate more optimal processes based on necessity, experience and desire. This is exactly what needs to happen in our society in order for us to experience true evolution and in order to fully realize our potentials as human beings, individually and collectively.

Therefore, in order for us to evolve and truly have money work for the human race rather than making the human race work for money, we need to let go of some of the false ideas (and/or values) that we have been taught to believe and that actually hinder us instead of helping us to evolve. In order for some people to accept and make use of the simple solutions expressed in this book, and the simple reality that will make them work, may require these people to let go of some of their old thinking about money so that law makers can act in favor of the human race instead of continuing to maintain the status quo.

We have been fed many falsehoods about money that keep our minds locked into the thinking that causes unnecessary suffering in our lives and in the lives of others. These falsehoods can be easily exposed and many of them are exposed in this book. We have the capability through the changing of some laws and agreements to create for ourselves virtually any kind of economy we like. It is time that we use this powerful capability to change the world for good.

In order to further prepare our minds for the solutions, I think that it is necessary for us to examine facts that dispel the untrue voices and ideas that would have us believe that there is great risk in adopting these simple solutions. The way that I like breaking the conventional and false thinking about our current global economic systems is to provide example after example of how silly, arbitrary and abstract the current system actually is and how much the current monetary system depends on our faith in it. It is merely the desire for the money we use to retain its value that continues to keep the system going. Once we truly grasp the concept that it is our desire alone that creates value, then we can accept in mass, perhaps for the first time in history, that our money is not in danger of being devalued provided that we simply continue to use it normally no matter what happens. This simple valuation of money can be mandated by law, as has been successfully done in the past. So before we unlock the solutions let's look at the futility of some of the more interesting and major monetary transactions that occur today.

Part 3

The Futility of Current Global Monetary Policies

We exist in a world where the United States Dollar is the most commonly accepted and used means of international currency. Even though, debatably, the United States no longer has a free market system, the US is often heralded as the proof that capitalism is the best basis of government. So let us take the U.S. dollar as an example of how money is created today, and we will then assume that most other governments use similar means.

I am going to simplify the birth of new U.S. dollars as much as possible, because, for the purposes of this book, it is only necessary to provide the basic construct in order to understand the arbitrary and abstract nature of the process and its fundamental flaw.

First, let's look at why we would need to create more money in the first place. Consider a simple example of what would happen if there were only $100 USD in existence and the entire population of the U.S. was only 100 people. In theory there would be $100 cents that could be equally distributed to each person. Next consider what would happen if, over a period of a year, there were now 10,000 people added to the population by various means such as births, immigration, etc. It would no longer be possible for each person to have 100 cents at any given time even if they were to attempt to earn the value of the money in some way, and thus an immediate imbalance occurs.

This example illustrates at least one practical need which may necessitate the creation of more physical money. This example also illustrates at least one practical problem, as previously discussed, that makes it impractical to use physical gold as a currency, or even to make paper money that is redeemable by the government in gold, because there is simply not enough to go around for all the countries and people in the world. Money backed by precious commodities is still essentially only another manifestation of money whose supply would need to be manipulated in some way in order to deal with these kinds of practical problems. Given the fact that we can design money by law in any way that we like, why can't we come up with a better idea? I believe we can.

Most people know that U.S. dollars exist in paper, coins and on balances in financial accounts. Yet most people have no idea where the U.S. dollar really comes from and how new dollars come into existence. Most people simply acknowledge that the U.S. is powerful with a military that can defend the value of a U.S. dollar and thus we give credence to the U.S. dollar and accept it as valuable for financial transactions. This belief holds today even though dollars are not redeemable by the U.S. Government for any kind of precious metal or anything else of value. It is tradable for commodities, goods and services, but not redeemable for many reasons, which have already been analyzed.

There are fundamentally two processes that result in the increase of the supply of money in the U.S. economy and both cases depend upon debt in order for money to be created. In the United States it is said that all money is backed by debt, which sounds good or bad depending on if you are a creditor or a debtor. So whenever new money is created, somebody has to repay it. In the beginning I believe that the idea for the debt implementation was based on the intention that the supply of money could expand and contract as needed. However, today the system of debt based money has proven inadequate to deal with the practical needs of the majority of people as demonstrated by the current state of global economic affairs. This includes high taxation, high government budget deficits, bankruptcies of government, disparity between financial classes, dependence on unreliable investment practices and cyclical economic booms and busts.

The first process of creating new money occurs when the U.S. Treasury issues its own bonds. A bond is the same thing as a loan agreement with specific repayment terms. So when a bond is sold by the U.S. Treasury the Treasury is borrowing money from the purchaser of the bond and eventually the Treasury must repay the money borrowed with interest. Those who purchase bonds expect to be repaid according to the terms of the bonds and there are several different kinds of bonds that are sold. When a private investor like a pension fund or the government of China buys a bond then there is no new money created, however, when the U.S. Federal Reserve Bank (the Fed) buys these government bonds it pays for them in newly printed cash. As stated in a quote from a Federal Reserve publication entitled "Putting it Simply:" "When you or I write a check, there must be sufficient funds in our account to cover the check, but when the Federal Reserve writes a check, there is no bank deposit on which that check is drawn. When the Federal Reserve writes a check, it is creating money." Thus this new money is literally created from thin air. The Fed is a private association of banks that is free to operate on its own within the framework of some limited U.S. Government oversight. Although it is said that new money is created by the Fed in these purchases of U.S. Treasury bonds it is important to remember that this "new money" is supposed to be repaid to the Fed. Thus the money created by the Fed is actually not "new money" but is actually new debt or temporary money at best.

The second scenario in which new money is created occurs at the local bank level. At the local bank level, all new money is loaned into existence. So this is also not really new money either but it is also really credit or new debt. At the Federal Reserve level, money is created out of thin air and then exchanged for government debt. In both cases, the money is backed by debt that must be repaid with interest. It is interesting to consider that under this system each year enough new money must be loaned into existence to cover the interest payments on all of the past outstanding debt.

Each year all the outstanding debt must compound by at least the rate of the interest on that debt and therefore each and every year it must grow by some percentage. Our debt-based money system grows exponentially by its very design and so the amount of debt in the system will always exceed the amount of actual money.

Outside of these two conventionally advertised methods of money creation there is the creation of money that comes from known and unknown economic events such as the 2008 financial crisis wherein the U.S. Federal Reserve (along with the national banks of other countries) simply purchased failing investment products from both U.S. and non-U.S. banks and investment companies in order to save the entire global economy from crashing. Essentially the Fed simply tried to capitalize debt by giving money out in exchange for questionable investment products. According to the first ever publicly available audits of the U.S. Federal Reserve $16 Trillion was allocated to corporations and banks internationally, purportedly for "financial assistance" during and after the 2008 fiscal crisis. This was one case that is now known to have happened. As a result of this new information I speculate that there are also likely to be many other cases where money is created and spent by the Federal Reserve. I strongly suspect that the Fed, acting either independently or by secret order of agencies in the U.S. Government (or even other businessmen or shadow figures), may create new money as needed based on situations that arise that are considered as related to national security or global security or other necessity (including personal gain). I think that it is reasonable to assume that these probably necessary but potentially unpopular issuances of new money are unreported to the general public because they are classified at a high security clearance level or otherwise not recorded anywhere

where they can be found.

For the purposes or our calculating the global money supply in relation to the ideas put forth in this book, the activity of the Federal Reserve since 2008 in buying commercial investment products represents yet another supply of money that may at any time be injected into the economy. As such this potential to create new money to avert financial calamity must also be taken into consideration when estimating the total amount of money that is really in use at any time.

I propose that, when trying to calculate the global supply of money, it appears by recent historical examples to be necessary to include the current perceived value of investment products as well as the margin that may be in use by all individual and institutional investors. This is because at any time, in order to maintain the stability of the lifestyle of the majority of the population of the world, you may have to monetize these abstract account balances. To me this necessary action by the Fed is an obvious sign that there is simply not enough actual money to go around in our economy and this exposes one fatal flaw in our system. I don't think that this is something that was foreseen when the U.S. fiat dollar was initially implemented in the 1930's. I don't think this is something to be embarrassed or worried about either but rather something that can and should be confronted and fixed. In this book I provide several methods to solve this problem. There may also be other ways.

Again to restate the issue in the simplest terms, the U.S. Federal Reserve and U.S. Government felt it important to monetize the investment products (and other debts) held by major global investors during the 2008 financial crisis in order to save the global economy in and after 2008. As a result the Federal Reserve (in cooperation with the U.S. Government) felt that it was necessary to buy these failing investment products with newly created money. Thus, I say that when we calculate the global money supply, we must also take into consideration the perceived value (or current account balances) of everyone's investment accounts as well as the (borrowed) margin that is in use by investors because at any time these balances may cause the issuance of new money into existence.

The fact that these investment account balances can arbitrarily be required to be monetized for whatever reason really goes to show that there really is not enough money in the float of the world in order to meet the minimum necessities of every person in the world. Since there is not enough money to go around it results in an economy of lack. This leads to a majority of the people suffering because of self imposed faulty economic practices and monetary systems. It is a shame we put ourselves through suffering over something that can be easily fixed.

Market capitalization is calculated by taking all of the shares of businesses and of investment products that are traded on public stock markets and multiplying all of these shares by their price per share. The market capitalization of a specific business or investment company is often thought of as the total value of the company as expressed by investors. As of 2014 the total market capitalization in the United States of all publicly traded shares was estimated to be over $20 trillion USD. By the end of 2013 the global market capitalization of the 58 major stock markets reached a new record of $63.4 trillion USD. These figures do not include market capitalization of investment companies, mutual funds, or other collective investment vehicles (simply because I can't find anyone who incorporates those products into the calculation). For the purposes of this book the account balances and market capitalizations of these kinds of investment products should be included in the calculation because they represent a perceived value as a balance in the brokerage accounts of the people who are invested in these products. This includes things like the S&P Index Funds and the Dow Jones Industrial Funds. The best estimates that I can find from the Investment Company Institute state that as of 2012 the Total worldwide assets invested into mutual funds is $26.8 trillion USD ($19.5 trillion USD coming from U.S. retirement plans alone). I find it interesting that the total market capitalization of the U.S. as computed by the World Bank is about $6 trillion USD less than the amount of money estimated to be invested in investment funds. That simply tells me that the best estimates of our economists are off by trillions of USD.

Let me throw another interesting caveat into the mix that also illustrates the arbitrary nature of the U.S. dollar and that also provides evidence to support the implementation of my solutions. I say that there is another way that the equivalent of U.S. dollars also gets created. The Chinese government has locked the rate of exchange of its currency (the Renminbi or Yuan) to the U.S. dollar for years. Thus, you can also assume that whenever the Chinese government prints money equivalent large number of U.S. dollars are also being put into global circulation. The Chinese can do this because they have enough U.S. dollars being sent to their country each year by the U.S. to buy goods and services that they can exchange dollars using their currency at whatever rate they like. The Chinese can also sell dollars against their own currency at whatever rate they like.

It is also interesting to note that the Chinese government has its own national debt which as of 2014 was $21 Trillion USD compared to the USA's $16 Trillion USD. In November 2010, at a meeting of the Russian Prime Minister and the Chinese Premier, it was announced that Russia and China have decided to use their own national currencies for bilateral trade, instead of the U.S. dollar. This is in order to further improve relations between Beijing and Moscow and to protect their domestic economies during the "Great Recession." The "Great Recession" was not qualified in the press release as the 2008 recession and thus leaves the question as to whether or not the Chinese and Russians are expecting yet another recession. The trading of the Chinese Yuan against the Ruble has started in the Chinese interbank market. Since the Chinese currency is fixed against the dollar and the Chinese are now trading their money with Russia, most likely within a fixed range, then it seems to me that the Russian Ruble could also be riding on value of the U.S. dollar indirectly. If this is the case then the creation of new Rubles also represents the creation of some U.S. dollars and *vice versa*.

Chapter 11: How Much USD Exists Today

If you research how many U.S. Dollars exist today, you will find a variety of responses from various government and financial institutions. In my opinion the reliability of virtually all of the calculations and information presented is questionable simply because each private, corporate and government institution that provides such information is motivated by their own agenda which influences the data. A very simple example of this is the fairly recent revelation by the Federal Reserve that it purchased over $14 trillion USD in failing investment products. Facts like this would never even been known before except that the U.S. recently passed laws that required the Federal Reserve to disclose presumably accurate information about its inner workings by means of audited financial statements that were previously never disclosed. I say presumably accurate information because I speculate that there would be no way for anyone to know if any information about money issued by the Federal Reserve was suppressed as part of any programs related to matters of defense or national security spending.

If the Federal Reserve issues trillions of dollars to help stabilize the economy, can we write off the possibility that money has and is issued from time to time to pay for U.S. Government or covert operations? As far as I am concerned the actual amount of USD in existence today is irrelevant to the majority of people who use the fiat money. I also believe that under our current systems in order to maintain the stability of any fiat currency it is in the best interest of its government to keep their estimates of money in circulation a secret. To do otherwise is only an invitation to undermine the thinking of people in regard to the entire money system.

For example, in the face of obvious evidence that

suggests otherwise, the average person on the street actually thinks that the less money that is in circulation the more valuable the money is. Therefore, it would appear to be in the best interests of the U.S. Government and its associated agencies to provide conservative estimates of the amount of physical and electronic monies in circulation. This policy of keeping the money supply as small as possible would appear to be common sense for the majority of people who do not understand what fiat currency is all about. On any given day you can find countless debates in the media from people who actually believe that the sky is falling because too much currency is being printed.

So before I provide my own estimate of the amount of USD that exists today, both electronically and in physical form, it is only fair for me to share with you my own agenda, which influences my calculations.

What compels my estimates of the US money supply? <u>It is my personal opinion that our current economic policies, popular beliefs and constraints have created a grossly inadequate supply of money in circulation, unable to meet the basic need to sustain a healthy life for either the people in the United States or for the rest of the people of the planet. To put it simply, there is not enough money to sustain a healthy global economy.</u> This is why our entire planet is constantly in a self imposed and unnecessary pattern of economic instability that creates false starts followed by oscillations of recession and depression.

Our entire economic system, and the uncertainties that it creates, places an unnecessary burden of perpetual worry and work onto the majority of people. It has been this way for a long time and I believe it is primarily attributable to nothing more than antiquated beliefs and traditions passed down through generations. System justification theory is a theory within social psychology that states people have a motivation to defend and justify the status quo, even when it may be disadvantageous for the greater good. Today, we live in a mode of system justification where we are in perpetual defense of our false thinking. I believe that wrong thinking has infected society and this wrong thinking can be changed at any time by simply exposing the falsehoods and thereby annulling the diseased thinking.

As a direct result of the most popular economic and monetary policies we have intentionally and falsely led ourselves to believe that the less money that exists the more valuable it is. Therefore those in charge of our monetary policies are motivated to continually understate the amount money that is actually in existence. I believe that both the intentional as well as unintentional provision of this false information creates even more economic instability no matter how well intentioned this policy of under-reporting of money may be. This is because it is thought by some that use of fiat money requires people to believe in the value of money and every time the economy collapses it undermines confidence which in turn creates more instability. In my opinion part of the solution is pure and simple honesty.

The laws of the government can provide for the value of the money if the country is relevant in the world. It doesn't matter how much money is really in circulation as long as people continue to believe

71

that it is in their best interests to use the money. Therein lays the real value of money. The real value of money depends on an agreement between people and nothing more. There is no stronger agreement than the force of law to back up the agreement. This agreement between people combined with the force of law underpins the value of the USD (and virtually every other major fiat currency). And so all we need to do is to alter the agreement slightly. Passing laws would be the best method to effectuate rapid and positive change for all people. There are also other ways to implement the required changes without the cooperation of government which I will share in subsequent sections of this book.

So, with my opinions having been stated, let me provide for you my own crude estimates and the most common numbers that you will run across when you ask how many USD are available.

By historical convention the amount of USD in the world is measured by "M" numbers, M0, M1, M2, M3, etc.. The U.S. Federal Reserve uses M1 and M2 as a standardized way of defining money in the economy. M1 is all coins and currencies in circulation, plus balances in checking accounts, travelers checks, etc. M2 is M1 plus short term liquid assets, like savings deposits, time deposits, certain CD's, money market deposits and money market mutual funds. M3 includes all of M2 (which includes M1) plus large-denomination ($100,000 or more) time deposits, balances in institutional money funds, repurchase liabilities issued by depository institutions, and Eurodollars held by U.S. residents at foreign branches of U.S. banks and at all banks in the United Kingdom and Canada. For whatever reason, since 2006, M3 is no longer reported by the Federal Reserve. Looking at a slide from a recent U.S. Federal Reserve presentation it looks like there is about a modest $11.29 trillion USD that comprises M2 as of July 2014 (M1=$2.79 trillion USD).

But then we have to consider money created from lending. This amount of money created from lending is related to a term called the Money Multiplier. To understand the Money Multiplier look at it this way, banks make their money by lending out more money than they have on deposit. As of 2012, according to U.S. laws, U.S. banks with less than $12.4M USD on deposit don't need to keep any amount of money in reserve when they lend, while banks with deposits of more than $12.4M USD but less than $79M USD need to keep at least 3% of the money that they have on deposit and can loan out the rest and banks with more than $79M USD must keep 10% of the total amount of money deposited in reserve and they are free to lend out the rest. So in the case where a bank has $100M USD on deposit, they can lend out $90M USD (they can actually lend out more if they borrow from the Federal Reserve itself, but that's another story). So if we just go with the numbers provided by the Federal Reserve in regards to M2, then the total amount of money that can be lent out based on M2 would be about $9.1 trillion USD. According the U.S. Federal Reserve as of December 2013 there were total deposits in US banks was $11.5 trillion USD and total loans were $7.8 trillion USD.

Next there is the U.S. budget deficit wherein the U.S. Government has an accumulated a debt of over $17 trillion USD plus interest, and, considering that M2 is $11.5 trillion USD, I'm going to be ultra conservative and assume that the M2 did not include ANY of the U.S. debt and thus the U.S. national debt will be added to my own computation of the amount of USD that exists in some format.

In my calculation I will also include the $14 trillion USD that the U.S. Federal Reserve used to buy investment products after the 2008 financial crisis.

Then there are the less tangible but equally important sums of all the investment account balances from brokers and funds and such. While it's true that these balances don't necessarily represent actual money, as I've already pointed out, they may very well need to be monetized by the U.S. Federal Reserve at some point, perhaps to avert a global loss of investors' money resulting in unimaginable economic disaster. So again, according to the World Bank the total market capitalization in the United States as of 2014 is estimated to be over $20 trillion USD. And according to the Investment Company Institute in 2012 the total worldwide assets invested into U.S. mutual funds is $26.8 trillion USD.

Finally in my analysis I want to come up with some estimate of the entire margin that is in use today by all U.S. traders. For the purposes of simplifying this discussion, let's just think of margin as all of the money that is created when brokerage firms lend money to traders to cover the purchase of investments that they could otherwise not afford to buy. For example at the time of the writing of this book it is not unusual for futures and even securities traders to be able to make investments that are as much as 100 to 1000 times more valuable than the money that they have in their brokerage accounts. Because of the difficulty in finding estimates of the total amount of margin being used at any time by investors using U.S. dollars as a basis (including securities as well as futures firms), and based on my own experience in trading and public markets, I'm going to be conservative and I'm going to estimate the total leverage being used is going to be about equal to the total market cap of the U.S. equity markets.

I strongly suspect that the real amount of margin being utilized every day is in the hundreds of trillions of USD because of the futures and currency margin options available at the marketplace today. There is greater risk in how margin is used in the currency markets than people realize. However, as a currency trader, I'll give some respect to the concept of how the term margin is used and represented in the futures currency markets as simply a range within which someone can trade with an amount of money that they have in their account. And because there are theoretical safeguards in place (strict margin calls) I'm not going to include all of this in my calculation of the total margin in use because it would blow things up to astronomical numbers. In other words I'm going to be very lenient and conservative in my estimations of the amount of money to include as margin.

Because the futures market trading in one day is about $400B USD, I'm going to simply multiply this by 50 in order to estimate the total margin in the U.S. on any given day for currencies as well as other futures. In regards to the stock market, I'm simply going to say that for the $20 trillion USD estimated market capitalization there is an additional $20 trillion USD in margin or other kinds of borrowing taking place on those securities, whether it be for the purposes of more leveraged trading in the markets or for down payments on tangible property. So my grand total for margin in use is $40 trillion USD which I believe is grossly underestimated.

Now before I give my crude estimate of the all the USD currently in existence in physical notes, or otherwise existing as a balance on an account statement (electronic or physical) let us be clear on what I am doing here. I realize that I am mixing years on some of this data, however, I am simply taking the most recent estimates that I can find and am happy to add those together just to give some insight as to what the total amount of USD might be in various representations today. For my purposes it is not necessary to be exact or even to be correct because there is no way for any of the readers of this book or for anyone else to come up with an exact number for the total USD represented in the world today either. What I am trying to do is to provide you with some things to think about based on various data available (that I consider to be suspect in the first place) and that often appears to be contradictory depending on the sources of the information. So this is not intended to be an exact representation but rather some numbers that will hopefully drive home the futility in arguing about the amount of money in the float at all.

So here is my estimate of the amount of USD in the world as of the writing of this book:

MONEY IN SUPPLY	AMOUNT		NOTES
M2:	$11.29	Trillion	(Physical cash and bank accounts, etc.)
Bank Loans:	$7.80	Trillion	(Money created from retail bank loans)
US Debt:	$17	Trillion	(money created by US government loans)
Federal Reserve:	$14	Trillion	(Purchases of risky investments post 2008)
U.S. Stock Market Capitlization:	$20	Trillion	(Balances in securities investment accounts)
Mutual Fund Balances:	$26.80	Trillion	(Balances from Mutual Fund products)
SUB TOTAL:	$96.89	Trillion	(Estimated Accessible USD Money Supply)
Investment Acct. Margins:	$40	Trillion	(U.S. Futures, Forex & Securities Margin)
TOTAL:	$137	Trillion	(Estimated. Perhaps much higher.)

So why is this estimate so important? What if, for the sake of argument, I had told you that there was actually over $900 Trillion USD in the float in the USA, instead of the $18 Trillion commonly referenced by the Federal Reserve? What impact would any of these numbers have on your life? The answer is that it would have absolutely no impact on your life at all. That is exactly why the subject of how much money is accessible in one form or another is unimportant. However, there is at least one practical reason why the actual supply of money versus the number of people is important to consider as a subject but I will address that issue later.

For the time being what is most important is for you to just consider that whether I told you that there is $900 Trillion USD manifest in some form or another, or $9 Trillion, it would not effect on your ability to go and acquire and spend money today. Regardless of your thoughts about the amount of money in supply, you as an individual will not influence the buying power of a dollar and it is unlikely that you have any desire to influence its value negatively. What would be the point in attempting to devalue the money? If you depend on the value of a USD like a great majority of the world does then why would you want to diminish its value anyway?

None of the estimated amounts of the money in the supply can be confirmed with any degree of reliability by anyone, so if you don't believe my estimates, then why choose to believe any other estimates? After all everyone has their own agenda when it comes to calculating the supply of money and exactly how much they want taken into consideration. Even if you could know the exact, correct amounts, these numbers are not what creates the value of the currency. So now I hope you find it as sad as I do to see all of the time that is wasted by pundits arguing over these numbers on the news and in government. These fictional amounts are only as relevant as you can trick others into believing in them. The only thing that creates the value (or purchasing power) of the money is the fact that people are willing (or forced by law) to accept USD in exchange for goods and services.

I want you to remember this discussion the next time that you watch people arguing over the idea that printing more money will somehow bring the sky down upon us. That may be true for some smaller, less influential countries but not for major countries like the United States. The devaluation of the currencies of modern countries typically requires that other countries stop accepting the money regardless of how much is in the float. The secondary reaction is typically the rapid printing of more money to solve the problem. Thus, the simple act of printing more money does not necessarily precipitate the decrease in the valuation of any currency in the global market place. The world is too heavily dependent on the currencies of certain nations in order for these currencies to fail simply because the supply of money increases. It is not as important to know the exact amounts of money in circulation as it is to know what the effects are of having too little money in circulation.

Chapter 12: Interest Paid on U.S. National Debt

Let me say that as of 2014 there is always a real threat of the U.S. dollar being devalued at any time due to a panic or other crisis. The biggest threat to the U.S. dollar and all other currencies is that currency exchange rates are not bound by any treaties and thus exchange rates are open to electronic attack, manipulation and fear mongering. Barring some kind of unforeseen manmade or natural disaster I don't think that there is much likelihood of a catastrophic devaluation of the U.S. dollar for many years to come unless it occurs as a result of pure fear and panic and it is important to realize that there are those people who are actually interested in creating such fear for their own profit. I do believe that if the U.S. dollar were to suffer a catastrophic devaluation it would not be because of the more popular contemporary arguments such as the high national debt or because of the notion that there is too much money being placed into circulation.

There is much clamoring these days about the buying power of the USD in relation to the national debt. There are many arguments regarding the tax burden that is being placed on U.S. tax payers to pay off the debts being accumulated by the U.S. Government. As I will explain in other chapters our entire taxation system is as antiquated and unnecessary as the idea that the government has to borrow money in the first place. The argument of greatest relevance to me in this chapter is the typical one that an increase in a countries national debt is somehow going to cause a lower valuation in its fiat currency. As of 2014, these arguments are losing traction as the national debt increases to record proportions and the value of the U.S. dollar does not appear to be diminishing as fast as the debt is being accumulated. One reason for this is that other major countries are also experiencing large national debts of their own in one form or another because they all continue to use the same inadequate and antiquated monetary systems. Events such as the 2008 global financial crisis really served to show how closely related all of the countries are. So if you take into account the increasing deficits of countries like China, and various countries in the EU when compared to the USA, it would appear that we are all in the same financial boat, and as a result the net effect is for the valuation of everyone's currency in relation to each other to stay relatively the same. After all why should China or the EU's currency be worth more than ours when they have the same or worse debt problems?

Then there is the argument that inflation will go up if there is too much cash available. The fact is that inflation will rise regardless of the amount of money in supply. In addition, virtually all of the studies attempting to measure inflation are unreliable as they are all so contrived to fit the viewpoint of those who create them that they are not even worth referencing. The fact is that we don't need to see any studies about inflation in order for us to 'feel' the results of inflation and know that it is an ongoing part of virtually every economic system. I will discuss my opinion on the more obvious source and nature of inflation in another chapter and some potential ways to cope with the problem that will still exist no matter how healthy any economy.

The U.S. national debt is a subject few people understand. There is not really any new money being created at all by the Federal Reserve's activity in lending but rather only a temporary expansion of the money supply. The Fed's portfolio of Treasury debt is its primary source of income. It is important to understand that when the Federal Reserve lends to the U.S. Government, the majority of interest that is paid to the Federal Reserve is returned to the U.S. Treasury. Essentially, the U.S. Government receives virtually all of the Fed's annual profits, after a statutory dividend of 6% for member banks' capital investment is paid. For example, in 2010, the Federal Reserve made a profit of $82 billion and transferred $79 billion to the U.S. Treasury.

So, while the Federal Reserve bank does make a profit from lending to the U.S. Government, the majority of that profit is turned back over to the U.S. Treasury. Some argue that the profit retained by the U.S. Federal Reserve may be too large compared to other privately owned businesses and that may be the case. I look at the profit paid to the Fed as just another expense that would otherwise end up being paid to some organization via our current system of income tax for performing the same critical tasks, such as check clearing, etc, that the Federal Reserve does. My point is that the relevance of the Federal Reserve's relationship to our money supply is that it does not actually increase money supply permanently but only temporarily.

The U.S. lending process simply creates debt that must somehow be repaid and this has been and continues to be a problem, on many levels, with our entire money and economic system. I contend that there is simply never enough money to go around for everyone to live with even a minimum quality of life that is hoped for in most modern countries today. Sure, there are many people who read this book that can say that they have a job that pays the bills and so there is no problem. But that is just it; until a problem arises that causes people to lose income through no fault of their own, like the coal miners in Kentucky, most of whom lost their jobs in and around 2012 for reasons beyond their control. The safety net for such people is a few unemployment checks, then food stamps which are not enough to maintain their standard of living. What people forget is that there is no certainty in the economy tomorrow that will provide jobs to enable all people to live a healthy lifestyle even if every person is willing to do good work. Not every person has what it takes to own their own business and even if they did there would still not be enough money to go around.

None of the solutions to the global economic stabilization that I present in this book require that the Federal Reserve be dismantled or that it remain in place either. I consider the existence of the Federal Reserve to be a topic for some other book and prefer not to disturb or disrupt the job security or money making schemes or threaten any establishment in order to effectuate the real and positive changes that I suggest. I would rather have their support than their opposition and I would think that it would be in the Federal Reserve's best interests to support my suggested plans because in the end they would still make money and it would help solve a problem that they are already trying to solve when they expand the money supply through investment bank bailouts.

Although I cannot confirm the thinking of the decision makers at the Federal Reserve I would think that they have realized the problem of there not being enough money in supply a long time ago. They certainly appear to take every chance they get to expand the money supply in ways that will last as long as possible. Considering the problem of the lack of money supply, I would not even fault the Federal Reserve for secretly giving money away in order to help deal with this substantial and long term problem.

Chapter 13: Countries Buy Each Others Debt

Another issue that is relevant to the discussion of money supply, and one that is often debated on mainstream media, is the issue of how much of the U.S. debt is owned by other countries. There are only two reasons why I find this discussion pertinent. The first reason is because it re-enforces the concept that there is not enough money to go around. The second reason is that it helps defeat the false notion that the less of our fiat currency exists the more valuable it is.

Again, let's use the U.S. national debt as an example. In September 2014, the U.S. national debt was estimated to be over $17 trillion USD with China financing roughly $1.3 trillion USD of this debt. The U.S. Federal Reserve (the Fed) owns the majority of this debt. As discussed, most of the profit and interest earned by the Fed gets paid to the U.S. Treasury. But the interest paid to China, and anyone other than the Fed, is just money that will need to come from somewhere to give to China. China may or may not choose to hold onto that money when it is paid back and thus if they keep it they will further constrict the supply of U.S. dollars available for use in the world. This is scenario is significant because it represents a potential slowing of the spending of money. This is not good in the global economy where I contend there is not enough money to go around in the first place. At least if the interest is paid to the Federal Reserve most of it will be returned to the U.S. Treasury where we know it will be spent by the U.S. Government. We have no such guarantees that anyone else who is paid interest from U.S. Government bonds will re-spend any of the interest or the principal paid to them. Some bond holders may choose to simply keep their money when the bond is repaid.

Now consider this next interesting caveat that illustrates the futility of our current constraints on the supply of money. We are led to believe that when countries such as China and Brazil purchase U.S. bonds (debt) that they are using the U.S. dollars that they have stored in their banks that have arrived in their hands as a result of exchange of currencies due to trading goods and services across borders. Supposedly, any country that wants to buy U.S. debt would need to get U.S. dollars to pay for the bonds. If they don't have enough money in their own reserve banks, then they would need to purchase U.S. dollars from the global markets by trading their own currency (or some other currency) for U.S. dollars. Such a large purchase might push the value of the U.S. dollar up on the global markets. All of this is good and fine, other than the fact that interest paid to these bond holders would not end up for use by the U.S. Treasury again, which isn't so great. Also, as principal and interest is paid out to foreign purchasers of U.S. bonds, so the U.S. dollar may weaken on the global exchange as other currencies may be purchased if they choose to divest some of their U.S. dollars.

Now consider a situation where a country needs to exchange a great deal of its own currency for U.S. dollars to make the purchase of the U.S. bonds. What if the exchange of currency occurred between the U.S. Federal Reserve Bank and the target country? Technically speaking, if this happened there could very well be a simple exchange of some other currency for newly created U.S. dollars. In other words one country would print some of its currency (or create it electronically) and send it to the U.S. who creates some U.S. dollars to send back. This transaction would equate to a simple exchange of one set of paper for another. In other words no value would be exchanged but new money would come into existence literally out of thin air that would never need to be returned. The U.S. Federal Reserve would then sit with large quantities of foreign currency in electronic or paper format that it exchanged for U.S. dollars. Although I cannot confirm or deny that such a transaction has ever taken place, I would find it hard to believe that it has not. It does illustrate that the only real value to the fiat currency that we use today is the utility that we choose to assign it and it is not based on any tangible economic indicators and certainly not on any commodities. This is a point that I will keep driving home.

There are many conditions that can cause inflation. The most catastrophic type of inflation occurs when countries devalue the currency of another country or choose not to do business with a particular country for whatever reason. The case of Zimbabwe is an example of this catastrophic type of inflation and devaluation of currency starting from 1991 through 2009. Economic sanctions imposed on Zimbabwe by other nations eroded the value of the currency of Zimbabwe. Zimbabwe eventually abandoned their national currency as a result. When this kind of catastrophic devaluation of currency occurs, it is normal for large amounts of money to be printed and injected into the market. However, the money is perceived to be worthless even though it may be easy to obtain. It is much harder to devalue the currency of a larger country such as the U.S. in this manner because currencies from larger countries are much more interwoven into the global economy. There is very little will for anyone to devalue the U.S. dollar when virtually everyone relies on some kind of trade using US dollars. To devalue the U.S. dollar would have a negative impact on virtually every country in the world and would not be in the interests of anyone significant.

I believe that the inflation that is of most relevance to ordinary people comes primarily from two causes. The first source of inflation is caused by a lack of money in circulation and lack of the availability of money for the majority of people to spend. Simply printing more money without distributing it does not help to fix this problem. The second greatest cause of inflation is our human nature that wants to get something in exchange for nothing. I believe this latter condition is exacerbated by the fact that the majority of people actually have had something taken away from them and unconsciously they know this. The majority of people being born today have already had their right to access and use property taken away from them at birth because of property ownership and systems of government going back centuries. So I speculate there is an unconscious tendency to want to get something back in order to keep things fair. Deep down inside those who are born into poverty as well as those who are born into wealth and everyone in between awareness exists that something is not right or "fair" because of the effects of economic inequality. This inequality is not created by any mysterious force or by God but rather it has been caused by our own collective failure to modify our economy to compensate for this problem. I am not in favor of making everyone financially equal but I am in favor of providing some compensation to those who are not born into wealth in order to help improve the quality of their lives. I also believe that the imbalance that exists subconsciously reduces respect for the authority of government and causes resentment against government and governments perceived lack of utility in the lives ordinary people. Fixing these problems could help restore faith in government that is conducive to pro-social behavior.

Inflation From Money Tightly Held

First let's look at the inflation resulting from lack of money or when money is tightly held or otherwise tightly concentrated.

The utility of rules derived from the study of economics is questionable over any given period of time because the study of economics is heavily dependent on human behavior. Human behavior dictates the conditions imposed on an economy by the laws of the ruling governments of the world. Because the behavior of people can change dramatically over time the laws, rules and regulations that govern economics can also change. For all of the above reasons the rules used in the science of economics are not static and they are subject to change. Because of the changing behavior of people and governments over time the rules and equations derived from the study of economics may be good for one period of time and found to be obsolete at later points in time. Some economic rules used by government to make key decisions are often flawed from the start and the problems are only realized after the damage is done.

In this way the utility of the theories and equations of economics is unlike the utility of the equations of science of physics where the rules of physical universe do not change. This is not to say that there is no utility or necessity in the study of economics, but rather that we must be careful to continually review and subject the "rules" of economics to scrutiny in order to ensure that they have not changed. We must acknowledge the possibility that following the "rules" may not always produce the expected results.

One of the greatest fallacies of the application of the science of economics that still pervades popular belief and hinders us to this day is the idea that placing more money into the float results in higher levels of inflation. The justification for this argument involves confusing the cause and the effect. To this day you will find economists that use this untrue thinking as a reason to connect high national debt with inflation. I argue that history demonstrates again and again that it is not the abundance of money in the economy that causes inflation but rather the lack of money in supply.

To prove my point one need only look at the great depression in the U.S. (1929-1939) as an example and every other recession that has occurred in the U.S. since. During the great depression people literally could not access their money because banks would not cash out the money that was in their accounts and so people could not spend. Let's look at an easily verifiable rule of Macro Economics that is so easy to understand that I accept this rule on faith. The rule simply states that when demand is low, suppliers must increase their prices in order to make a living because less of their products are being sold. Apply this obvious principal to the time of the great depression. Buying things like food became hard during the onset of the great depression because money was hard to come by for the majority of people.

During the days leading up to the great depression the U.S. national debt was not of any dominating concern. Let's use the price of food as a popular indicator of inflation for the purposes of our discussions. The fact that there was literally no cash available from banks that were crashing and jobs lost meant that less food was being purchased and so the prices of food had to be raised by farmers and distributors in order to keep themselves in business. My point is that there are clear examples that individual lack of supply of money precipitates inflation. Lack of money usually precipitates an increase in national debt not the other way around. One of the most important cures for the great depression was for the government to spend money on jobs programs. Because fewer taxes were being collected the government needed to borrow money for the jobs programs and government deficits increased. So the lack of money came first, then the inflation, then the national debt, not the other way around.

Similarly, look at what happens during a recession, when money is tightly held and jobs and incomes are scarce. Again food suppliers must raise the cost of their food because less is being purchased. And, as a consequence of money being tightly held, the government must borrow money (increase the deficit) in order to stay in business. Less tax revenue is being collected because less money is changing hands. So it is not the case that more money being borrowed by the government lowers the value of the money or increases inflation, it is a simple matter of not having enough money in the system in order to encourage people to spend money and buy more.

Without money changing hands there simply is no economy. It seems simple, yet many economists miss these obvious relationships and as a result they often preach misleading ideas to the public and policy makers. Many people have been indoctrinated in thinking that an increase in the supply of money that results from deficit spending is a bad thing when in fact it may be the only source of cash that keeps the economy afloat. It's like saying rain attracts clouds rather than acknowledging that a rain cloud generates the rain. When the government chokes off its services and payments to people during times of poor economic conditions the results are harder economic times and even higher perceived inflation. This has been demonstrated by the devastating effects of austerity policies adopted by governments such as Greece in response to their own deficit and to the global economic crisis that started in 2008.

These facts are no secret to those who run the U.S. Federal Reserve, whose reaction to recession or depression is to lower the interest rates. By lowering interest rates the Fed is encouraging banks and lenders to put as much money as possible in the hands of as many people who borrow and spend it.

When the Fed and the government take action to stimulate the economy by lowering interest rates or creating jobs or welfare bailouts some refer to it as Keynesian economics. I tend to think of these actions as common sense. If more people have more money to spend, the more they spend it and the healthier the economy. If no-one has access to any money to spend (i.e. money is being tightly held) then there is no economy at all. The biggest problem is that we are still using an antiquated system to supply more money temporarily. The very problem that caused us to go off of the gold standard in the first place was inadvertently re-engineered into our current system because of our lack of experience and maturity about what creates value of money. We simply traded one commodity for another. The current system can never be made to permanently correct the problems that exist. Our current economic and money supply systems are inadequate to deal with the problems we are faced with and thus the entire system is destined to fail again and again by virtue of its design.

Today the only solution that we have to put more money into the system is for banks to lend it into existence or worse "invest" into risky endeavors.

As we have seen in recent years banks act in their own self interest, and this can result in reckless practices. Ironically the very reckless lending that helped to temporarily bolster our economy in the past eventually led to the real-estate and financial bubbles and a major international financial crisis. In turn, as a result of the economic crisis, banks are now being told that they were lending money too easily to too many people who were not able to repay it. So the banks have been punished and told not to lend so much money and to be more scrupulous in the amount that they lend and to whom they lend.

Oversight is all very good except for one monumental problem. The problem is that the only tool that currently exists to put money back into the hands of people to spend in order to stimulate the economy and repair it is to lend more money into existence. But how can banks lend sufficient money into existence whilst their hands are being tied by new regulations, and they are being punished for their loose lending practices.

So it appears that we may have an ongoing no win situation. The only other means currently available to put money into peoples' hands to spend using our severely limited and antiquated monetary system is for the government to spend money on jobs programs and social welfare programs. Thus the government must engage in deficit spending to save the economy, which it is doing and creating the largest deficits in history. Now most people have been taught to believe that deficit spending is bad and no-one really knows what is going to happen when the deficit gets too big for us to pay using our tax systems. We could implement some kind of crippling austerities, as did Greece, but if you take away the government jobs programs, food programs, medical programs and other government spending then you have no money to put into the hands of the people and, without enough jobs to go around, you have an unhealthy economy.

To summarize my point, the proof that more money needs to be given to people to spend is all around us. The U.S. Federal Reserve uses one of the only antiquated tools of debt creation that they have to help fix the economy by lowering interest rates and their publicly stated goal is to make cheap money available to everyone. Even as we take interest rates closer and closer to zero the problem is still not going to be over particularly since banks are under more scrutiny than ever in regards to their lending practices.

Those who run the U.S. Federal Reserve know that the only way to rebuild a broken economy is to put money into the hands of people to spend, but a lower interest rate is not adequate. At some point after 2008 the system failed to such a degree that the Fed actually had to resort to an unorthodox measure i.e. purchase failing investment products in order to get more money into existence. I say that this was good and the U.S. Federal Reserve must not be afraid to engage in any other unorthodox activity that may be necessary in order to get this much needed cash out where it can be spent so that we can continue to have a dynamic economy.

The situations described in this chapter highlight some of the problems with our system. So what now? I say we start over with something new and fresh. It is time for us to make slight adjustments to achieve a system that is designed to succeed rather than stick with senseless systems that threaten the welfare of everyone that uses them and the very stability and security of the entire world. We need to stop playing games and taking unnecessary risks by continuing to use these monetary supply systems that have proven again and again to be disastrous. We need to stop pretending that there are no solutions to the problems when the solutions are right in front of us.

Again, it all comes down to the actual amount of money in supply. If there is not enough to go around, then it actually becomes more worthless. The evidence provided proves that there is not enough money in the current global system to capitalize the lives of the citizens of the developed countries, much less the citizens in all of the developing countries.

Inflation From Disparity & Desire

There is another kind of inflation that comes from the desires of people. There is a tangible imbalance of wealth and property that currently exists in that the majority of people are not properly compensated for the use of the land and resources that are automatically denied them at birth. It is a core concept of this book that under our current system some people are automatically disadvantaged in order for others to have adequate or plentiful financial means. One of the exacerbating features of this is that there simply isn't enough money to go around. It is also a core concept of this book that there are equitable solutions to the problem. Whether or not you like my solutions there is no denying that the current system persists for the simple reason that we have not decided to change what is within our power to change. There is no excuse for inaction when solutions exist that do not hurt anyone or take anything away from anyone.

So am I advocating the unwinding of our entire system of money or that wealth be distributed equally? No. I think that the use of money still makes sense unless we can come up with something different. An imbalance of financial means is natural. What my solution involves is to simply elevate the quality of life for those who are poor for whatever reason. I advocate restoring something to each person that has been denied by the status quo. I advocate providing a modest compensation for use of life sustaining property that is no longer naturally available to anyone because of our modern implementations of government and law.

The manifestation of imbalance that is inherent to our system of property protection is that most people eventually come to point where they realize the futility in attempting to work hard for something that they should already have. What they should already have is the right to occupy and share land without having to pay for it. Remember if it were not for the construct of property rights and our existing governments that protect those rights by force, we would all have equal access to the land and we would all have equal opportunity use land in order to survive as did the Native

Americans before us. No matter how much people enjoy their jobs and enjoy working very hard this imbalance created by the existing system persists and the system forces some to the bottom as others accumulate more.

As a result of this imbalance people are unconsciously encouraged even more to seek some value that they feel that they are entitled to and that they would otherwise have. If the problem of the imbalance were to be corrected in some way people would still have a tendency to want something for nothing, but I it would be less of a problem because they would not be in such extreme need.

We are encouraged and programmed to save for retirement. Retirement is some day that you can finally do what you really want to do without having to work (for money). Your physical health may be diminished by the time this day comes and you may need that retirement money to pay for increased medical bills. Our generally accepted programming for retirement requires a mindset that says, "I need to get some kind of return on investment for my savings or I need something more than what I am currently earning". We are programmed to live for the future and thus many live less for today.

As direct result of our need to get something for nothing we create the classic "bubble" where cash flows into investments, like property, stock markets or gold in much the same way it flows into a casino or a Ponzi scheme. Even buying bank CDs carries risks these days because of the instability of our banking system. The majority of people want to put their money somewhere and magically have much more returned to them than they put in. In other words we not only want something for nothing we actually need it because of the way retirement works out in our society.

Some investors say they are being paid to take risk and some might even say they do their homework but that really doesn't compensate for the fact that there is only so much money to go around in the first place. Again, we have the problem of not enough money to monetize all the investments especially when you consider that the population keeps growing while the money supply is static (only the debt supply grows in our current monetary system). Thanks to technology and global connectivity money flows back and forth from the stock markets to property related investments in faster and faster rotations around the world.

People expect to 'flip' properties and other assets within increasingly shorter periods of time for ever greater profit. But why should we expect to be able to do this at all? Why would anyone expect to sell a house for more money than they put into it in the first place? There is a phone book of answers to this question to justify this common investment expectation. However, in the end there is really only one reason for the recurrence of these investment bubbles other than greed. The majority of people need a return on investment.

People believe, because they need, there is somewhere where they can put their money and get more back for nothing. Many people who are first into these vast market bubbles make money in this way at very fast rates adding credence to the entire investment concept that forms the basis of a bubble. However, the money that is used to pay profit to those who are first into the pyramid will eventually come from the many more people who invest into the bottom of the pyramid. Once the bubble (or pyramid) is sufficiently blown up to a big enough bubble, then major economic instability results and money becomes tightly held for a period of time that we call a recession or depression. The limited few at the top of the pyramid of an economic bubble that actually make money before or while the bubble bursts, hold onto their money and profit because they see the hard times coming. Then we have recession, followed by inflation followed by deficit spending until those holding the money let some loose into the next bubble. Eventually they will have to let some money go in order to make more again, but this process of letting go usually takes time.

The ongoing inflation that is experienced in large first world countries, such as the U.S., is a byproduct of two things; lack of access to money for spending and peoples' strong desire (or requirement) to get something for nothing. Contrary to popular opinion inflation is certainly not coming from the rapid devaluation of the U.S. dollar by other countries. Other countries are not motivated to damage the U.S. dollar and their monetary value has no reason to be significantly greater compared to the U.S. dollar because they suffer from the same economic problems.

If we cure the problem of people not having money human nature dictates that we will still have a tendency to want something for nothing and there will still be people who want to participate in investment markets. However, I contend that where people do not feel the pressure of needing to save for retirement or the desperation of day to day survival, there will be smaller investment bubbles. In addition, because investments will be more heavily monetized rather than depending on leverage, the impacts of bubbles bursting will not leave people without a way to pay for their rent, food, medical, education and transportation. In other words the effects of investment bubbles will not be as catastrophic if money continues to be available for spending. <u>We would experience a much more healthy economy even during a depression if people still had money to spend from a guaranteed source of income.</u> At the very least the lifestyle of people during a depression would be better if they had some monetary income than if they had none at all.

Another Remedy for the Effects of Inflation

Inflation is not the same issue as the price fluctuations of commodities such as oil and metal that occur based on supply and demand. Inflation is a side effect of human behavior and perceived necessity that results in increasing prices. Once prices are increased due to inflation, for whatever reasons related to inflation, they are seldom ever decreased. Inflation is something that we will have to deal with under any system that uses money because it is based on human behavior.

The problem of inflation is so pervasive that ultimately we may find that the only cure to it is to actually reset the value of the units of money periodically through acts of law. As an example of what this would look like imagine if a simple law was passed today in the U.S. that required that all dollars printed before a specific date will now be reset to a factor of 1/10 and all prices of goods and services must be lowered accordingly. So based on this solution a 100 dollar bill printed yesterday would only worth 10 dollars today. Bank accounts with 100 dollars in them would be reset to 10 dollars. And all prices quoted today, would by law be reduced by a factor of 10. This example shows a simple potential solution to overcoming inflation and restoring the perception of value to a currency. After all perceptions, including perceived necessity create inflation in the first place so why not use perception to fix the problem.

However you choose to deal with inflation I contend that the most important thing is that people have money to spend in order to have an economy.

To summarize this section, I contend that more people with more money to spend (whether they are given the money or earn it) helps to create a good economy which leads to a slowing of inflation. Furthermore I contend that there are other simple and practical means to deal with inflation caused by human behavior.

Part 4
A Better Monetary Policy

The only truly valuable and precious commodity in the world that is critical to any economy is the human being. All other commodities are simply inanimate objects without any economic value at all unless human beings assign value to them. Because human beings are the only creatures that assign economic value, human beings are the only commodity that is the source of any economic value at all.

At the time of the writing of this book the economic stability of the entire world, along with everyone's ability to retire someday, relies on the stock markets around the globe. These stock markets and the shares that are traded in them are an abstraction. The stock market is essentially a casino where popular opinion dictates the value at which shares of various companies are bought and sold every day. It is the goal of every investor to sell an investment product for a higher price than the price that they paid originally. They must realize as high a profit as possible in as little time as possible (the amount of time involved in the transaction being relative to the thinking of each investor). Rather than get into a discussion about all of the various specific types of investment products being sold throughout the world, let's look at shares of businesses because these are the types of investments that ordinary people hear about every day and into which most people look to invest. Let's refer to businesses as public companies since they have shares that are traded on stock exchanges. The public stock markets, such as the New York Stock Exchange, are also usually private or public businesses with shares that are owned by people.

In most cases when someone buys shares of a public company the purchaser becomes entitled to one or more votes per share in the decision making of the company. The more shares that are owned by a single person or group of people the more votes they can cast towards decisions of the company. In addition, there is the understanding that if the company were to close down its operations and sell all of its assets then the money derived from this sale of assets would be distributed to the shareholders, thus each shareholder is said to own a "share" of the business. Some companies pay their shareholders dividends from the profits that are left over at the end of each year. Some companies do not pay dividends but their share price increases as a result of the perceived value of the underlying business. The concept for the value of shares that don't pay dividends is that, if the company was to shut down today, the accounts receivable and the assets that would be distributed to the shareholders would be significant enough to make the shares worth their current price. For more specific information about publicly traded companies and investments please read my book from 2005, "Financial Markets and Technical Analysis".

This all sounds logical, but in many cases the price paid for shares of any given companies have almost no relationship at all to the asset value of the company or of the profit or loss of a company. In many cases there are very big publicly traded businesses that trade far above and far below what their fundamental financial statements tell us about the health of the company. In the 1980's it was popular for 'sharks' to find companies whose shares were traded at prices that were so undervalued that if the company were shut down, all the assets sold and accounts receivable collected paid out as distributions to share holders would yield a significant profit per share. In these scenarios the 'sharks' would do what was called a 'hostile takeover' of such undervalued businesses by buying enough shares at a low price to gain enough voting control to force, by virtue of their majority vote, that the company shut down, sell its assets, and distribute the profits to its investors. Performing hostile takeovers is no easy task these days and is not done as often as it once was.

Today we are more likely to find companies whose shares trade well above what their net asset value justifies, and well above what could ever be collected in accounts receivable if the company were to go out of business. In this way, I have come to look at the stock market as a big horse race and investors are gambling in the same way as you would at the racetrack. One significant difference is that in horse betting the casino (or house) usually takes a fixed percentage of the money from bets being placed and there is always money to be paid out. In the stock market if all of the stocks lose value across the board the entire capitalization of the market can literally disappear altogether. In this way gambling in the stock market carries with it more significant long term risks than betting in horse racing.

The values of the stocks that are traded in these global stock markets are important to ordinary people, including you and I, for many reasons. For one, our money is invested by banks either directly or indirectly into the market. For most people who can afford to have any kind of savings plan, the returns on investments (in order to provide for individual retirements among other things) are expected to largely come from these stock markets.

Even if you have no savings or any money in any banks, most of the businesses that we rely on every day are connected in one way or another to the stock market. One need only look to recent history to see just how important the value of investment products has become to our entire way of life. The economic failures experienced throughout the world in the recession starting in 2008 were a direct result of investment products related to real-estate and lending becoming worthless for a period of time. The crisis was so great the U.S. Government, along with other first world governments and their associated reserve banks, actually had to step in and purchase these failing investments from large investment firms. Extraordinary action was taken by various governments in order keep the investment banks (that hold peoples retirement money as well as money from various trusts and pensions) from collapsing completely.

So what does all of this have to do with solving the global economic problems? Very simply put, the stock markets that we have all come to rely upon and that we are all encouraged to invest into with the associated and potentially devastating effects on our global economy, also holds the key to our ability to attain economic freedom and stability. All that we need to do is to utilize the same generally accepted notions that create the perceived value in individual stocks in the stock market and apply them to the money supplies of the world. As we've already discussed there are many stocks of companies that trade at values much higher than is justified by the analysis of their financial books.

Take the banks that needed to be bailed out by the government during the financial crisis. What makes these businesses so valuable that they need to be saved no matter the cost? What causes the perception of the value of a share of a company? Fundamentally, the share value of businesses that trade on the stock markets of the globe depends on the following factors:

1. The value of the tangible and intangible assets of the company, including customer base, brands, etc..
2. The receivables, revenue and profit of the business.
3. The perception of the future value of the business.
4. The perceived ability for the business to get something accomplished.
5. The necessity and relevance of the existence of the business (i.e. too big to fail, needs to exist, how does the existence of this business benefit us?).

Today the currencies of the various countries are traded in global foreign exchange markets between governments, banks, institutional and individual investors. These currencies are traded in much the same way as stocks are traded in stock markets.

The only difference is that no-one can tell you why the British Pound Sterling can be traded for 1.63 USD dollars. Using physics we can explain the behavior of the force of gravity, but there is no person that I'm aware of that can tell you the origins of the force of gravity and why it behaves as it does. Similarly, no one can say definitively what the values of various currencies should be in relation to others based on any tangibles such as the amount of gold held in Fort Knox. On any day we can say that the price of the US dollar is up or down in reaction to certain events, but no one can say definitively why these specific exchange rates exist in the first place, nor is there any attempt by any leader of any country to step up and definitively state why a specific currency should be stronger than another.

It was a relatively recent event in history that the U.S. and other major countries became heavily dependent on the fiat currency model and abandoned commodity based currencies. Commodity based currencies have proven unsustainable and throughout history they have inspired hostilities between countries that had unequal commodity supplies. At the end of WWII the Bretton Woods Accord was established. This was an international agreement that allowed currencies to fluctuate within a 1% range of each other. It was the Nixon Administration in the U.S. that ended this agreement and thus began the perilous practice of allowing, and even encouraging, currency rates to fluctuate without any specific constraints in global markets. The unbounded fluctuation of the prices of currencies contributes to the concern over increasing global economic instability and uncertainty that we experience today.

The potential devaluation of the U.S. dollar is the fuel that fires countless unnecessary political flames and plays a role in economic instability perhaps more significant than any other mechanism that exists today. We have the power to put an end to the instability by simply re-instituting currency exchange rate control agreements. In this respect I believe China is not the enemy of the U.S. economy that they are often made to be, but rather China is simply ahead of the problem by realizing that fixed currency rates are a necessity in a world that depends on fiat currency.

Rather than referring to China as a currency manipulator we really need to be following their lead by seeking to lock in currency exchange rates rather than risk devastating devaluation for no good reason. Until formal arrangements are made to fix the problem of floating currencies the best thing that all of the developed countries have going for them is that there is no political or business motivation to devalue any of the world's major currencies. I believe that it would be foolish to assume these comfortable world conditions will last forever. A simple act of terrorism or a natural disaster on a large enough scale could cause this delicate dependency on each other's currency values to unravel. Even errors in computers that are used in international currency trading or unscrupulous behavior by right currency traders in major banks could conceivably have catastrophic global effects. It is not worth it to leave these kinds of financial disasters and unknown devastating potentialities to chance.

Within our current circumstances and in our global

stock exchanges lay the both the problem and the solution to achieving global economic stability. When a viable business whose shares are traded on the stock exchange needs money management simply issues and sells more shares of their business to investors in the market. This includes businesses that are profitable and those that are losing money and require more capital to stay in business. Whether a company is famously profitable, or whether they are losing money but are still relevant, people purchase the shares due to the perceived value of the underlying business. Most investors are not buying shares of companies because they are backed by gold or any other commodity but they are buying them because of a perceived value. In some cases the value that is perceived boils down to nothing more than the relevance or the necessity that the business survives, as in the case where the banks and brokerage firms were rescued after the 2008 financial crisis because they were 'too big to fail.' In the cases of the investment banks that were almost bankrupt, relevance and necessity sustained their business and ultimately led to higher share prices.

If the investment banks were allowed to fail in 2008 then the results would have been catastrophic to everyone and may have included consequences such as loss of life due to the disruption of the basic provisions of goods and services. Imagine people walking out of managing a nuclear power plant because there was nothing valuable to pay them with or because they were unable to get money for food. Our economy that depends on the money supply is directly tied into the critical infrastructure of our day to day lives.

This is the only real reason why the US dollar lives today and has taken on a necessary utility and sustainable value. In this age the successful maintenance of the existing infrastructure including transportation, energy, medical, military, food and distribution, and technology is required in order to sustain our lives, and the dollar is at the core of virtually all of these critical infrastructures. If any one of these critical parts of our global infrastructure were to fail millions of lives would be lost. Whether people like it or not the entire infrastructure is facilitated through trade of money, primarily U.S. dollars. Even changing the primary currencies being used could cause disruptions in the provision of goods and services around the world depending on how it occurred.

In order to solve the problems of the individual counties themselves and the global economy at large the countries of the world need to start valuing and issuing their currencies in the very same way as public companies do with shares. In order to save the world, we must abandon the practice of issuing money in exchange for debt only.

Instead countries need to start treating their currencies as shares of any other business and valuing them based on the same fundamentals as that of stocks (without the same voting rights). If you want to use any commodity to back up any currency then the only commodity that makes sense is human lives. Human beings are the only creatures that associate value with money and use money to trade for goods and services. Human beings are required in order to have any economy in the first place. Because human beings are the actual creators of the value of money it stands to reason that we've been valuing the US dollar and every other currency before it based on incorrect standards. People alone make the dollar valuable. It is the choice and will of the people who use dollars that make dollars useful in the first place.

Even a person who never works a single day in their lives is valuable to the economy in the sense that they are consumers who spend money to buy food and other necessities required to sustain their lives. Even those who intentionally do no work and remain poor stimulate the economy in some way. They are consumers regardless of how or where they get their money or supplies. In fact, by using the value of items that are sold today you can literally put an average estimated economic dollar value on a human life. By simply taking into account the cost for the average person to pay for rent, food, electricity, communications, transportation, I think that you will find that if a person in the U.S. lives within a minimum standard for 50 years then on average about $1.5M will have passed through their hands, either directly or indirectly, in order pay for the necessities of life. This is based on medical care, education and everything associated with the cost of living being about $3,000 per month for an individual. So we can estimate that even the life of a 'couch potato' is worth $3M US dollars if they were live for 100 years.

It gets even more interesting. As already discussed, according to the readily available data on the internet the total amount of US dollars estimated to exist in all formats is not more than $30 Trillion USD. **Using this $30 Trillion USD figure there is not enough to money in existence capitalize the lives of each**

individual in the U.S. population with even $100,000 for their entire life (assuming a population of 312,000,000). Even if you use the larger estimated amount of money existing in all formats that I put forth in my analysis which is $137 Trillion USD, you can still only capitalize each U.S. citizen with just over $430,000 USD and most of that money is either tightly held and exists as an electronic account balance. Given the concentrations of money known to exist today, these numbers indicate that no matter how good the economy performs it is simply impossible for every person in the U.S. to save even $100,000 USD for their retirement because there is literally not enough money in existence to place in everyone's account no matter how hard they work. Given these numbers, how could it be possible for all of the people in the United States to live out the "American Dream"? There is simply not enough money to go around for the majority of people to even live stress free lives let alone own a house and cars. We've called it a dream for so long when in reality, because of our monetary system, it is actually an "American Fantasy". The instability caused by our money system causes rapid changes in our economy more and more frequently resulting in a lack of money even for those people who are willing to work hard.

The solution to the problem is not to tax the rich to death and re-distribute wealth. We've tried that for years now and it only inspires more anger and resentment. Creating a society based on communism where everyone is economically equal by decree of law is also uninspiring and unpopular for many reasons.

Thus far capitalism has demonstrated the greatest

utility and popularity to facilitate equitable trade and property ownership for the human species. Participation in the capitalist system is perceived to be passive. It is also perceived as the least intrusive to the day to day lives of people, whether or not that is actually true. I believe that for now the system of capitalism should remain in place as we seem to have nothing better. The only problem is that the system of capitalism by itself is merely a framework in which we divide property and effectuate trade of goods and services and thus the use of the capitalist system by itself cannot fix the current problems of our global economy. In order to fix the problems of poverty, availability of resources and global economic stability we need to make slight changes in laws and treaties that govern things such as money creation, money valuation, use of money and access to money which have implications on the use and availability of resources for everyone.

The problems we face are not insurmountable problems to solve at all. In fact, they are easier to solve then you might think and the validity of some of the potential solutions are already being proven directly and indirectly by current events.

The following is a simple list of things that I propose that should be done in order to solve global economic problems that we have been facing for years. Implementing the components of the simple plans provided will cause an immediate increase in the standard of living for everyone in the world, even those people who live in countries that do not immediately subscribe to the program.

This simple plan is not based solely on my own ideas. Some ideas and parts of the plan such as currency rate controls were used before with varying degrees of success due to the specific implementations (the Bretton Woods Accord). Some of the concepts I endorse have been suggested and endorsed long ago by the founding fathers of the U.S. including Adam Smith. In addition there are many supporters of the proposals given in this book throughout the world today including citizens of countries like Switzerland who have made serious proposals that would require the government to provide a monetary stipend to all its citizens. For those who favor such concepts as a resource based economy, I believe that the models proposed in this book would eventually help to facilitate the transition to better resource management out of necessity and provide the capital to make such ideas possible.

In subsequent sections of this book I provide various implementations of a new monetary system that does not require any government to do anything new. However, I believe that the most optimal implementation would occur with the cooperation of one or more major economic superpowers such as the United States, China, France, Germany or the UK. Only a major international country upon whom the global economy depends could successfully implement the plans described in this section of the book. Smaller countries upon which the major economies of the world do not have significant dependence would most likely fail implementing the new money system unilaterally. That is not to say that a sufficiently large group of smaller countries could not band together to implement the plan, but major countries would ensure the success of the plan. The milestones that I will provide in this section describe a scenario where the United State leads the charge and implements the plan first, but any major country including the EU or even China could also be first to perform the implementation.

It is important to understand that the order of the milestones A, B and E are interchangeable and will not need to be implemented in the specific order given. This is important because the U.S. doesn't need any specific country's cooperation to take the steps below and as already discussed there is little will for anyone to stop using U.S. dollars anywhere in the world. In a subsequent chapter of this book I will illustrate how ordinary people can actually implement and achieve the same or similar net results without the cooperation of any of the governments of the world.

I will provide a list of the components of the plan then look at each step individually in more detail.

The fundamental milestones lead by the U.S. to create global economic stability and to provide for everyone are as follows:

A. DEFINE A NEW BASIS FOR THE VALUE OF THE U.S. DOLLAR

B. START ISSUING MONEY AS NEEDED TO RECAPITALIZE THE COUNTRY AND ITS CITIZENS

C. PAY THE CITIZENS OF THE COUNTRY A MONTHLY STIPEND (No need for income tax).

D. IMPLEMENT CURRENCY SUPPLY REDUCTION PROCEDURES (Optional).

E. IMPLEMENT INTERNATIONAL TREATIES GOVERNING CURRENCY EXCHANGE RATE BOUNDRIES (Optional but highly recommended).

Let's look at each component of the plan in more depth.

A. DEFINE A NEW BASIS FOR THE VALUE OF THE U.S. DOLLAR.

Through acts of law the country would declare a new standard for the valuation of money based on the assets and infrastructure of the underlying country including the default economic value represented by each individual person's contribution to the economy as a consumer and not as a producer (because not everyone is a producer and there is value in the economy from consumers).

At the core of the solutions that I propose is the fundamental concept that governments or other issuers of money value their money in the same way that a publicly traded company on the stock market values its currency. Governments would simply issue money as required in order to finance new infrastructure and capabilities in the same way that relevant businesses do today using the stock exchanges of the world. Why should we value a country and its currency any differently to any other business?

The reason that this will work is because it is already our generally accepted and long standing practice in each of the existing stock markets to value the shares of business using the following already discussed standards (in this case the shares of each country are their dollars):

1. The value of the tangible and intangible assets of the country, including customer base, brands, etc.. In this category no one will argue that the United States has tremendous value from both hard assets and capabilities including roads, infrastructure, military, medical, law enforcement, space exploration and countless intellectual assets, etc. The cost to reproduce these assets would bankrupt any country today. Indeed, the reputation and brand of the United States is popular and accepted by the majority of people worldwide.

2. Receivables, revenue and profit of the business. In this category the U.S. has the right to impose taxation on any or all of the people and businesses in the country. In addition the U.S. has direct authority to print money and lend it and charge interest. Under the new system the government, acting through the Federal Reserve or by itself, will have the right to lend money and earn interest on that money as well as pay for and collect life insurance policies on each citizen. Even though these kinds of profits would simply be returned to Treasury and even though the country may no longer have a substantial income per se, the country will always have unlimited authority to generate additional income at any time from every person and business that exists within the country. And using any conventional financial analytics this unique ability to harness any and all money at any given time makes the country and its shares (its money) more valuable than the market capitalization of all public companies combined.

3. The perception of the future of the business by the investment public. Based on this standard any country that has unlimited access to capital to build and produce has extraordinary future value. In fact, there may need to be laws enacted that constrain the government's ability to invest so as to continue to allow ordinary people to also participate in investments and share in the rewards.

4. The perceived ability for the business to get something accomplished. Again, based on the past history of the innovation and ability of the first world countries such as the U.S. why would anyone doubt this standard of value exists in any developed country.

5. The necessity and relevance of the very existence of the business (i.e. too big to fail, needs to exist, how does the existence of this business benefit us?). I believe that applying this standard is the most important analysis that really supports the argument that the U.S. need not obtain the permission or substantive cooperation from any other country in order to implement these new money policies. Just like the big investment banks around the world that were bailed out during the 2008 crisis, and considering all of the critical global infrastructure and the vast military capability of the U.S., any country that dared to intentionally devalue the U.S. dollar would not only destroy their own economy (which may depend on our trade relationships) but they would risk damage to critical infrastructure in the U.S. such as our ability to maintain infrastructure like nuclear power plants. Such disruptions could lead to the destruction of the entire human race. I don't think that there is enough ill will for any major country to take this chance. Considering how the Chinese treat the exchange value of money themselves they have no motivation whatsoever to devalue the U.S. dollar. In fact, China is already a world leader in the practice of currency rate controls. The other developed countries are likely to join us and change their economies accordingly given that they are plagued with similar national debt crises to that which we are experiencing in the U.S..

B. START ISSUING MONEY AS NEEDED TO RECAPITALIZE THE COUNTRY AND ITS CITIZENS.

The The key elements to this part of the plan are as follows:

- Immediately Issue enough money to pay off the national debt.

- Stop borrowing money and instead issue more money (stock of the country) as needed to pay for all government expenditures moving forward.
- Make use of price controls if necessary to ensure the stable transition.
- Permanently end income tax and possibly other forms of taxation because they are no longer necessary.

I believe that the above steps are self explanatory. The idea is simply to issue money as a public company would issue stock in order to capitalize and sustain operations. The underlying value of the currency would be established and enforced by law and, if necessary, using price controls. Temporary price controls have been successfully used in the past for various reasons on many items including limiting the price of oil to temporarily limiting the price of food items during wartime. A temporary freeze on all prices was used during the Nixon administration when the U.S. discarded the Bretton Woods Accord. Both directly and indirectly the Federal Trade Commission makes heavy use of price controls and heavily enforces claims of unfair pricing and business practices on a daily basis. There are many other examples of indirect price controls, including import taxes that are already in effect and have been used throughout the history of the country.

Again, the four things that will cause the U.S. dollar to retain its value while it is being issued in large quantities are:

- the necessity to issue the money,
- the force of law,

- the valuation of the dollar using generally accepted accounting methods and
- the will of the majority of the people in the United States and in the world that depend on U.S. dollars and desire to continue to use the dollar without devaluing it.

C. PAY THE CITIZENS OF THE COUNTRY A MONTHLY STIPEND.

Replace all social welfare expenditures with a single monthly minimum income payment to all U.S. citizens regardless of their residence and earnings. Some people may require a higher monthly benefit paid to them depending on their health and other extraordinary medical needs.

Let's look at a specific example of the benefits that would be associated with an ordinary U.S. citizen under my suggested plan. As of 2014 under the model that I propose a person would receive a Net monthly benefit payment of $1,620 USD from a total monthly benefit $3,700 USD that would be distributed as follows each month:

A. TOTAL MONTHLY BENEFIT paid for each U.S. Citizen:	$3,700	
1. Federal Tax Burden paid to U.S. Treasury:	($1,080)	** Optional (29%)
2. State Tax Burden paid to State of Residence:	($200)	Avg. 5% per person.
3. Health Insurance (automaticaly paid by Gov.):	($400)	
4. Life Insurance (automatically paid by Gov.):	($400)	** Optional
5. Balance of benefit paid to individual:	$1,620	
B. Example Personal Monthly Budget (over 18yrs age):	$1,620	
1. Rent	($500)	
2. Food	($400)	
3. Car payment (Transportation)	($200)	
4. Auto Insurance	($100)	
5. Feul / Maintenance	($200)	
6. Phone / Inernet / Communications	($80)	
7. Discretionary	$140	

NOTE: ** Optional; These are expenses that may or may not arise depending on how the entire system is implimented. I show them here for sake of being thorough.

Let's break down each expenditure from section A above, the TOTAL MONTHLY BENEFIT.

Federal Tax Burden paid to U.S. Treasury (#1): I say that this payment is optional because it could be eliminated entirely depending on how you want to limit or otherwise measure the federal budget. Instead of making this payment you could simply allow the government to issue as much money as it likes to pay for its expenditures and then keep the money received back by the government in life insurance the same. Under my recommended example system, the federal government could still issue and spend as much as it sees fit. I recommend issuing the money as part of an automatic payment from each individual to the government in order establish a budgetary benchmark. This benchmark could help to keep spending within certain boundaries that help keep other member countries in alignment with each other's spending and citizen benefits. Thus, while the amount of money printed for the government to spend on each person each month may vary, having some benchmark of this spending is a good idea. The fact is that there will most likely be spending by the government that is beyond what it receives from this automatic subsidized tax payment. Under this example model any additional money spent (or issued) by the government that is not recouped by the life insurance policy taken out on each person (see A.4) would be 'extra' money. This 'extra' money could remain in circulation permanently if no other measures were ever taken to remove it from the money supply. But this would be fine because this money would still be backed by the value of the additional assets, infrastructure and capacity that was created by its issuance, just like the value of shares are backed by the same measures for public companies on the stock exchange. Therefore, in the system that I recommend, I have included this payment in order to provide the government with some rational baseline spending limit targets. So the Federal Government will receive $1,080 per month for each citizen in order to do whatever is necessary to provide infrastructure and services to its citizens. Upon the death of each citizen the government will recoup the money spent on servicing that individual through life insurance policies (or other means that are discussed in other sections). In the example above I simply estimated the burden that each person represents to the federal budget based on standards existing in 2014.

State Tax Burden paid to State of Residence (#2): Most state tax liabilities are calculated based on the amount of Federal taxes being paid by each individual. In order to eliminate state income taxes the Federal Government will provide each state with a payment of $200 per month for each person that resides in their state.

Health Insurance Benefit (Automatically paid by Gov.)(#3): I have no desire to put anyone out of business by my proposal or to create the perception by any potential powerful adversaries that my plan will threaten their existence. Using my plan I see no reason for anyone's business to be negatively affected including the large health insurance lobby. Therefore, I propose that the government simply pay $400 for each person's medical insurance policy per month. In the case of someone who requires more medical service then we can either provide for a higher payment or continue providing such benefits as Medicaid to offset the burden that would otherwise be carried by the health care insurance providers. $400 per month should be enough to provide every ordinary person with 100% medical coverage without any deductibles. It is also important to consider that, because each person adds value to stimulating the economy by being a consumer, it is important that we protect the health of our consumers so they can continue to contribute to a healthy economy.

Life Insurance (automatically paid by Gov.) (#4): Recent to the writing of this book the U.S. Government is attempting to provide affordable health care to all of its citizens at great expense to the government. Considering the costs it strikes me as odd that the U.S. Government would not also look at the possibility of taking out life insurance policies on everyone who uses the program in order to help recoup all of the costs paid out in medical benefits over the lifetime of each individual. If you're going to subsidize the cost of medical insurance for all of your citizens then why not get something back in exchange for the cost? It seems an obvious solution to pay for a life insurance annuity for each person who receives these health insurance benefits. In this way when a person eventually dies the government could be repaid and might actually be able to make money rather than lose money. At the same time the life insurance industry which consists primarily of large investment firms could be infused with more capital to create more jobs and have more money to invest into the economy.

There are people who will still argue that even if there is not enough money in our current system to go around we should not print more money and pay everyone without finding some way to take some of the new money out of circulation over time. The life insurance policy that I propose is one means to achieve this goal. I don't pretend to know whether or not it will become necessary to remove any money from the system by returning it to Treasury and that is why I labeled this expense as "Optional." However, if we do take some measures to keep the money supply constrained by creating such mechanisms these methods should not become burdensome to anyone as is the current income tax system. I believe the simplest constraint on the money supply should be related to the number of citizens that are required to be serviced by the money in the first place. This falls directly in line with my standpoint that human life is the only commodity that makes any sense to use in relation to establishing the value of any currency. Consequently, I believe that at least one of the best mechanisms that could be used to shrink the money supply is to take out life insurance policies on each person to whom benefits are paid. In this way, whenever someone dies all of the money paid to them would be returned to the government and some or all taken out of circulation (retired to treasury).

Balance of the benefit paid to the individual (#5):
In addition to receiving health care benefits that cover 100% of each citizen's health care costs, each person would receive this amount via a direct monthly payment into their bank account (or equivalent cash card). This is the net amount of money that a person could use to pay for their rent, food and other essentials. This is not making anyone rich, but it is provided in order to compensate people for the use of the land and other property that they would otherwise have access to if we did not have government and property laws. Under my system, I propose that each person over the age of 18 be provided with this cash benefit for their entire life regardless of their income or existing wealth. I believe that everyone must be paid under this program whether they are rich or poor regardless of their resources because if you were to reduce peoples benefits based on their higher income it would create an artificial ceiling that would discourage people from earning too much more money for threat of losing their benefits. This is the very same dilemma that many people who receive food stamps and other social welfare face. Under many circumstances this dilemma does create a real

barrier of perceived potential diminished economic returns when you are on the threshold of obtaining a job that will do nothing but make you work more hours for a benefit that you already receive for free. Under my plan benefits for each citizen under the age of 18 years would be the same as illustrated above with the exception that half of their Net benefit ($810 per month) would be paid directly to the parents of the minor and the other ($810 per month) would be saved by the government until the minor reaches the age of 18 at which time this "savings" money (about $174,960) would be turned over to the young adult in one lump sum. This could be used for whatever they like, e.g. going to college, or establishing a home. If you wanted to, you could also make the receiving of this money after the age of 18 conditional on 1 or 2 years of community service. However, that could create other problems as some may decline and then we still have economically disadvantaged people.

Example of Monthly Personal Budget (Section B):
This is the use of the net amount of money that each adult would receive as part of their benefits each month. In my example I propose $1,620. This amount is not enough to make someone rich but making everyone rich is not the point. Perhaps there will be some people who will live their entire lives using this amount of monthly income to survive and they will be happy doing nothing but contributing to our economy and society by being a good consumer. Other people will not be satisfied with this small amount of money and they will use it as a tool in order to finance the building of great inventions or great new businesses that may make them wealthy. And when people become wealthy under this system they will not need to have their

earnings taxed to pay social security. Everyone will already receive enough income to live within a basic standard of comfort. Those who are not wealthy will at least have a chance to spend their time in the pursuit of happiness. Everyone will have the option to pursue their hearts' desires rather than being forced to spend 8 hours a day working at a job that they may not even like for an income that is hardly sufficient to meet their basic needs.

D. IMPLEMENT CURRENCY SUPPLY REDUCTION PROCEDURES (Optional).

We touched briefly on this component of my plan when I spoke about the life insurance policies that I propose that the U.S. Federal Government take out on each citizen. In this section we explore this and related issues in more details.

I contend that this step is optional because I have no evidence that taking steps to shrink the money supply are really necessary in my proposed monetary system. While I have no evidence I do believe that it is still prudent to put some mechanisms in place that also take money out of the money supply from time to time. The amount of money that is allowed to exist in the money system should depend on the number of people in the system. You can think of it in this way, human lives are the only commodity that creates any value for any currency. Without human beings, money is worthless and there is no economy. Therefore the amount of money issued and in circulation by a country should be related to the number of citizens being serviced. Thus, when someone is born and lives more money is placed into the system as needed (i.e. the monthly stipend) and when someone dies money should come out of the system (i.e. a life insurance policy pays money back to the government removing money from circulation as needed).

There are many methods that can be utilized in order to remove money from the system when people die (and even while people are alive) which we will discuss but one of my favorite methods is the concept of using life insurance policies. By using life insurance policies as a means to remove money from circulation you must also pay money out to life insurance companies that use the money to make investments and thus help further stimulate the economy. I am also hopeful that by suggesting the use of life insurance as a means for the government to recoup its spending on its citizens and their related infrastructure that I will gain the support of the powerful investment and insurance company lobbies in the adoption of my system.

Other methods to remove money from the supply that could be used in addition to life insurance include interest earned from lending by the Federal Reserve, estate taxes, property tax and import and export taxes. There may be other taxes that can be imposed by the government in order to help remove money from the system, but I am reluctant to recommend that the government levy any kind of taxes because I think that it is unnecessary and virtually all systems of taxation eventually lead to excessive taxing, costly bureaucracy, disenchantment, criticism of the government and in many cases abuse by the government.

Having stated my resistance to the use of any taxes to remove money from circulation, if taxes were to be used I think that the two taxes that make the most sense are estate taxes and property tax. Estate taxes collected by the government should be based upon and should not exceed the amounts paid out by the government to the individual that passed. People who are interested in avoiding this tax could take out their own life insurance policies to cover the cost of this kind of estate tax so that they could pass on their possessions to their loved ones should they die.

Using property taxes as a means to remove money from circulation also makes sense because the primary function of most modern governments is to enforce the segregation, use and rights of property amongst the residence of the country. Therefore it would make sense that those who choose to own property should pay the government a fee to make sure nobody else can take it away from them (as if anyone really owns anything in the first place).

The final method of removing money from the supply is to more firmly establish the mechanisms that enable the U.S. Federal Reserve to participate along with private local banks and lending institutions as the lender of last resort. In other words, allow banks of all sizes to lend out more money than they already do by borrowing more from the Federal Reserve. The majority of profits made by the U.S. Federal Reserve are paid to the U.S. Treasury, hence this money could be retired by the U.S. Treasury when collected. Therefore, the government would be able to shrink the money supply by engaging in the business of lending, or it can profit from the creation and lending of new money via the Federal Reserve which already lends money and pays profits to the government.

Before we end this section let's consider what the next 100 years would look like in terms of money supply if we were to issue the monthly stipend to people and then remove the money paid to them from the economy including some small interest. A spreadsheet showing an example of what this scenario would look like is provided in Appendix A. Insisting on an interest payment in addition to the money paid may not be advantageous or necessary in the long term; however, I put it into the analysis below for those people who might think that paying some money back with interest may be advantageous.

While you examine the table in Appendix A, consider this as a method to expand the money supply in order to capitalize the lives of each of our individual citizens so as to help everyone enjoy a basic standard quality of life, while also establishing a method to remove money from the supply of money based on population. Also, when you look at the table consider what life will be like if we continue using our current monetary system, including all of the unknowns and risks associated with running high budget deficits and not being able to sustain the services of education, law enforcement, military, welfare and medical programs for the elderly or anyone else because there is simply not enough money to go around under the current system of debt.

There may be other solutions. What other solutions would you propose?

E. IMPLEMENT INTERNATIONAL TREATIES GOVERNING CURRENCY EXCHANGE RATE BOUNDRIES (Optional but highly recommended).

There are those who will argue that this step should be done first. Some people will argue that without the agreements of other nations the entire plan will not work. I intentionally put this step last and made it optional because I believe that all other countries will be forced to accept our new system and sustain the value of the U.S. dollar or risk global economic disaster. I believe that by adopting the systems proposed in this book first we will strongly inspire other countries to adopt the same system for their citizens and join us in establishing currency rate boundaries. They will do this in order to protect the value of their own currencies as well as ours. Another obvious reason that it would not be necessary to obtain the cooperation of any other country in establishing our new money policy is because within the U.S. and its territories the value of the dollar itself is regulated and enforced by law. Which of the world's largest trading partners would be able to contravene U.S. laws within the borders of the U.S. and what would be their motivation to do so? The value of the U.S. dollar is under no risk of devaluation at all because its use and value is governed by force of local law.

It should also be noted that this is not a revolutionary idea that is designed to put any currency traders out of business, but rather this is a return to an upgraded version of exchange rate governance that was already successfully used to sustain values post WWII under the Bretton Woods Accords, and was only abandoned in the 1970's. Even though I am an avid currency trading enthusiast who has actively traded in the markets for a great deal of my life, I am not afraid to admit that the best possible scenario to help ensure the stability of the economy of the developed world would be to lock in currency exchange rates to as close to fixed amounts as possible. However, I recognize that global currency trading is also big business with big lobbies in the offices of our government and so, in order to gain the support of the powerful institutional traders and other puppet masters of the markets, I say that it is enough to simply establish upper and lower boundaries to the currency exchange rates. In this way those people whose careers and way of life depends on making money from the unpredictable fluctuations of the values of currencies can continue to do so under the new system. Having upper and lower boundaries for the rates of exchange of currencies should help prevent the risk currency traders face of losing all of their money at once because of the lack of boundaries that exists today.

I would even argue further that, because of the way that margin is so heavily used by traders in the global currency markets, failing to establish clear upper and lower currency range boundaries between the major currency pairs creates the highest possibility of the next largest global economic disaster. By failing to establish these boundaries we are inviting a global economic disaster from which we may not be able to recover. I call this scenario the "global thermal nuclear currency meltdown" where all currencies cease to have any value. It is irresponsible for our world leaders to continue to allow this possibility to exist by ignorantly supporting floating currency exchange rates without boundaries and resisting the policies of countries such as China, who actually recognize this problem, and are trying to maintain the stability of their own economy.

Earlier in this section I explained that if the U.S. were to implement these monetary policies that the U.S. Dollar could not easily be devalued by other countries without great risk to their own economies. However, there are some circumstances where the conditions can exist where the other countries could devalue the U.S. dollar and may even be forced to do so. Such conditions that threaten the value of the U.S. dollar on the global markets can occur if any of the technology around the markets of currencies ever malfunctions by accident or by intention. Other conditions that threaten currency valuations arise if the U.S. ever becomes distressed by natural disasters, acts of war or terrorism.

Within the U.S. law exist provisions that allow the U.S. Government to issue money as needed under extraordinary circumstances such as during a disaster. The problem is there are no international treaties between developed countries or NATO partners that require our allies or any other countries to uphold the rate of exchange of the U.S. dollar as may be required if such a disaster were to occur. A powerful enough disaster could affect the entire country and require the U.S. to purchase goods and services from outside of the country. If an emergency occurred that was so great that the U.S. could not solve the problem from within and needed to import resources from outside the country then as things currently stand the U.S. dollar may rapidly become worthless in the global market; too rapidly for us to make essential purchases. If the U.S. were sufficiently crippled then there may be no motivation for any other country to maintain the value of the U.S. dollar and thus the U.S. dollar may devalue faster than we could issue the money or use it for anything.

Considering the real threats that the world faces including climate change, extreme weather events, terrorism, internet warfare, economic warfare, outbreaks of disease, nuclear plant failures, nuclear war, meteorites and other unknowns, I believe that it is prudent to take precautions today.

I suggest that we form a new global currency association, first amongst either our NATO allies and/or the G7 countries, in order to agree on the boundaries for the rates of exchange of each other's currencies. Additional countries could be invited to participate to have their exchange rates sustained by the other member nations subject to certain conditions such as not developing nuclear or chemical weapons, or by requiring limitations on defense spending by new member nations. In addition, members of the council could vote to devalue other member nations' currencies if they break their agreements and they could even devalue or suspend dealings in the currencies of other non-member nations in order to help avert wars or other dangerous activities that threaten those in the currency alliance.

The potential for this currency association to help facilitate the transition from our current debt based monetary system to my proposed consumer based monetary system is obvious. Any member nation that elected to simply issue money as needed would be able to retain the value of their currency as a direct result of the agreement by the other member nations of the monetary association.

Obviously the monetary association would need to establish conventions that would govern the maximum amounts of defense spending within member nations and the maximum amount of individual benefits that a member nation could pay to its citizens. Member nations could choose to pay their citizens nothing and maximum benefits payments can vary from country to country, however I can see a need where member nations would have to find a way to keep one country from paying its citizens inordinate amounts when compared to other member nations. At the same time, some member nations may have special needs, such as extreme geographical and climate conditions, that require more flexibility for those choosing to live in those climates. The association could simply vote on a country by country basis if necessary without needing to establish any binding conventions in the early stages.

Similarly, the issue of defense spending would need to be addressed. For example, imagine if China wanted to join the currency association. Using my model the Chinese government would have the largest budget in the world due to their population so nothing would prevent them from becoming the largest military spending country in the world and creating the largest military force in the world other than treaties and conventions. This would probably be viewed negatively by the U.S. and its allies. The answer to this problem is that member nations of the currency association would have to come up with proposals to limit this spending amongst new members like China and all member nations would need to agree to audits and inspections in order to make sure that these agreements are being enforced.

There are those that would argue that being a part of such a currency association would amount to the member nations giving up their sovereignty. This is only true to the degree of suffering and lack of self sustaining capability a member country would have if they were to withdraw from the association. Therefore, this argument of forfeiting of sovereignty is an illusion of the mind. A country whose economy is capable of sustaining itself at any point in time could withdraw from the association without harm.

The problems occur when a country experiences internal duress and needs to be a member of the association in order to survive. A powerful country could always leave such an association and survive, but a powerful country sufficiently crippled by the very threats that we all acknowledge do exist would have no means to sustain itself if it were not part of a currency association. Membership in one or more currency exchange boundary rate associations is like having an insurance policy to help cover the costs of recovering from potential disasters. The U.S. could help to lead and establish such a currency association between its allies before another group of powerful countries creates a competing association of their own. I believe that China is already creating their own association by means of treaties and agreements that they are actively seeking with other countries to stave off currency devaluations that they perceive are eminent under the current system. Sadly, the U.S. and other countries are not yet willing to even acknowledge that a future potential problem exists.

It is in our best interest to join our allies in creating this mutually beneficial currency rate exchange association, and even inviting other countries including China until such a time as it becomes a burden. If it becomes burdensome to our national sovereignty then we can abandon participation in the association and allow our currency rate to fluctuate again as it does now. Given all of the reasons that I have outlined in this chapter, I think this currency association is a necessity that will serve us and not a luxury that we can afford to do without. Failing to plan for threats to our country and economy is irresponsible and every day we fail to act jeopardizes our national security and sustainability.

Chapter 16: Implemented Without Government

In the previous sections of this book I introduced the methods by which one or more of the most powerful governments of the world could make simple changes in their monetary systems that could end poverty, end the necessity for income tax and lead to a more stable global economy. The plan described would allow for the expansion and contraction of the supply of money based on the number of people in the country. The proposed plan would provide for the minimum capitalization of each citizen that would be required to sustain a minimum standard of living for everyone. The value of the money supply would be backed by generally accepted valuations used every day in the stock markets including assets, capability and relevance.

I believe that benefits would be most rapidly experienced by people if the plan were to be implemented by one or more major governments of the world. I also cannot see any people, party or businesses that have influence over the politicians of the world having any reason to oppose the plans I've presented in this book. Big business, the bankers, investors, commodities dealers, government, bureaucrats and the military industrial complex, as well as environmentalists and those interested in a resource based economy and ending poverty all stand to gain new income, new capabilities and new customers from using my plan. All parties concerned would make and keep their profits because there would be no need for taxes. No government or public institutions or jobs are threatened as the IRS could be absorbed into the Social Security Administration. The government incentives to purchase property and control peoples' behavior could be continued by keeping import and export taxes and by imposing other regulations and price controls as they already do. Even the intelligence gathering community would stand to gain new higher budgets to continue to gather the flow of information that it collects about people.

However, as Machiavelli said, "There is nothing more difficult to take in hand, more perilous to conduct, or more uncertain in its success, than to take the lead in the introduction of a new order of things." Therefore, in consideration of resistance from politicians that may arise due to paranoia, system justification or other unforeseen reasons I provide this chapter.

In this chapter I will introduce methods that would eventually achieve the same benefits and results of my monetary system without the government taking any initiatives. Having the cooperation of the government is the best solution in my opinion, however, there are a means to eventually achieve the same ends and the more people and businesses join into the processes I describe in the sections that follow, the faster everyone will reap the rewards and the more likely the politicians would get the message and eventually be inspired to usher in the monetary changes that I proposed in the previous chapters.

It should be noted that the implementations described in this section of the book are not a threat to any government or its powers. Implementation of any of the plans in this section would help to relieve the strain of the welfare systems on almost any government. The governments of the world could choose to assist and participate in any one of the following plans at any time and their cooperation would be welcomed.

The Private Company Plan Implementation (Including Non-Profits, Churches, etc.)

It is common practice for companies to take out life insurance policies on its employees where the company is the beneficiary. In most cases death benefits payments to the company are not taxable which creates a better return on investment than simply investing in annuities that are not related to life insurance. There is great debate as to the morality of such practices and in regards to the use of the proceeds from death benefits payments to the company particularly in cases where employees may not be notified that any insurance policy has been taken out on them at all.

As part of the implementations of some of my plans I advocate making extensive use of life insurance annuities in order to repay and even profit in the future from expenditures that serve people today.

The core of my plan is to provide as many people as possible with a minimum monthly payment for the rest of their life, in the order of about $1,600 net dollars after taxes according to 2014 standards. This income would provide the recipients with enough money to survive without being forced to take a job that they do not want or without having to worry about loss of the minimum amount of money needed to survive. They would not necessarily need to worry about the health of the economy and would contribute as consumers with money to spend and purchasers of life insurance investments.

The plan is simple. Any existing business or newly formed business, including non-profits and churches obtain the consent of their employees or contributing members to take out life insurance policies on them in exchange for some payment of benefits today or some other benefit.

In order to fully appreciate the model let's look at an example. An enthusiast of my concept decides to start a company by capitalizing it with $3,000,000 USD and then hiring people and paying them to do 2 good deeds per week. An already existing and profitable company would already be capitalized and could simply commit some of its profits to this process.

In the case of our example of a newly formed company the owner of the company agrees to pay 1 person a gross pay (including all employment costs) of about $2,000 per month for up to 100 years to work for the company. Again, the job is to simply do one or two good deeds per week and report them to the company. Each month the payment is made and after taxes are deducted the person receives $1,600. Each month a payment is also made to a life insurance policy on the new employee with a death benefit that would pay the company back an amount that is significantly higher than the total amount of all of the employee's paychecks over the period of 100 years. Alternatively at least enough benefit should be paid from the policy to repay what has already been paid to the employee thus far.

In our example let's keep it simple and say that the company takes out a life insurance policy that pays back $6,000,000 upon death and that this costs the company $500 per month. Assuming the person lived 100 years, the company would have paid the employee $3,000,000 and upon the death of the employee the company would receive $6,000,000 and could then expand its program to pay 2 people. If the employee dies before 100 years then there would be more profit that could be paid to the owner of the company.

What would motivate private companies to do this? Besides helping to build the economy and implement the plan, there is obvious profit that can be made by simply varying the numbers depending on how much you plan to re-invest into paying more people. In fact, I would strongly urge all businesses and churches to get permission from their employees to take out life insurance policies on them in exchange for some payment or benefit today even if it is only a nominal one-time payment. Imagine if enough businesses created variations of this plan that only paid people $10 per month or $100 per month. A person could receive multiple smaller benefits for life by working for multiple companies and performing virtually any kind of activity.

One of the only things that would need to be in place would be to remove the "idea" (stigma) that somehow taking out life insurance on people is morally wrong. Could there be abuse? Of course some business owners may try to kill people, but I think the overall majority those who people would benefit from these practices and whose managers would not try to kill them would by far outweigh practices that are already against the law and immoral. We do not abandon the practice of using cars even though thousands of people are killed in them every year and even though they are sometimes used as weapons by insane people. There will always be people who are sociopaths in the world but this is an issue that has more to do with genetics, education and environment then whether or not people use life insurance as a tool or weapon.

The Public Company Plan Implementation

The public company plan is just like the Private Company Implementation except that the business is capitalized by the shares of a publicly traded company. The public company plan implementation is one of my favorites for several reasons. The first reason is that use of life insurance on employees to generate profit for public companies is already a successful practice widely used by companies like JPMorgan Chase and Wells Fargo. The only difference between my plan and that of already existing companies is the use of the proceeds from the payouts on the life insurance policies. I also like the plan because it creates a profitable investment opportunity for people who believe in the implementation of the concepts that I present. And finally because the public company implementation allows for an unlimited amount of capital to flow into the business from investors and the stock market. The number of people who can receive a lifetime monthly benefit is limited only by the ability to sell more shares of the company.

The public company implementation plan goes as follows:

1. Form a corporation whose employees are hired to perform 2 good deeds per week.

2. Register shares of the company with the securities authorities to be sold to the general public. In the U.S. registration would be with the Securities Exchange Commission (SEC).

3. Once the company is sufficiently capitalized for at least the next 70 years per person from the purchase of its shares, the company hires as many people as its budget allows.

4. The company takes out life insurance policies on each of its employees and executive staff in amounts that will provide for substantial profits for the company when death benefits are paid.

5. Long before people die the life insurance policies themselves become valuable assets on the books of the company which can enable the company to sell more shares to obtain more capital and hire more people.

It's one of the simplest businesses that I can imagine and the investors actually have real assets and real value backing their shares. The stability of the insurance companies providing the life insurance policies is indisputable. They are practically immune from ever going out of business since the 2008 government bailouts proved that they were 'too big to fail' and the government will bail them out in times of economic crisis as needed.

Obviously, already existing public companies can create divisions to execute this same concept without having to do an Initial Public Offering (IPO).

Virtual or Internet Based Currency Plan Implementation

The final, most direct and simple implementation of my plan is to simply leverage the new age of virtual currencies. In countries where the internet is not available the currencies could be integrated and maintained by a community of people working within a multi-level structure where all transactions are cleared verbally or by cell phones if they are available.

In 2007, while living in Cape Town in the Republic of South Africa I was involved with a credit card processing business and a proposal to the government to create a new public private bank for the benefit of the people. While working on the business I wondered how it might be possible to create a new payment system that could be used anywhere in the world and that did not require a credit card or processing terminal. The system had to be so simple and reliable that even people in war-torn counties in Sub-Sahara in Africa could successfully utilize the system to make payments for goods and services. I came up with a model that could be used by people without technology but would really work well if ordinary cell phones where available. The model was based on the system used by organizations like the Knights Templar who acted as some of the first bankers.

The system and the new currency relied on human beings, which fits in perfectly with my model of a currency based on the value of human beings. I called the currency and the monetary system the "Dot" system. The units of currency were "Dots". I decided that I should arbitrarily assign the value of one Dot to be equal to the value of one British Pound Sterling on June 11, 2007 when I thought of the idea. In order to maintain the value of the Dot we would simply establish certain boundaries or price controls on the price of various commodities, raw materials and retail items in relation to the Dot and review and adjust them every 2 years or as may be needed.

The fascinating part of the "Dot" project arose when I decided that it would be advantageous to fix the exchange rates of the Dots in relation to other currencies. It was then that I realized that if people started using the Dots around the world then I will have unilaterally fixed the rates of all global currencies. Powerful indeed, but how could that be done? Well, it could be done based on the will of the people who decided to use the Dots. In other words if Dot users just agreed not to exchange Dots with other currencies for any amounts that were outside of the fixed rates then the system would work. What would motivate large institutions to use Dots as currencies? This is even more exciting to think about! I realized that people within countries like the DRC had the least to lose and also had so much abundant natural resources that they could force the utilization of the Dot. They would simply require that anyone who wanted to buy commodities from them do so in Dots. If a group of impoverished nations in Africa united to force the use of this currency, then it could be implemented on a large scale. Why would they do this? They would do this to implement and capitalize the very same currency based monthly stipend program that I am advocating throughout this book. This could end poverty not just in Africa but for any group of people who subscribed to use of the Dot and, in doing so, became eligible to receive a monthly stipend of Dots.

Another market of Dot users that would come to the table immediately would be those from the commercial banking sectors and currency traders who would buy Dots and trade in Dots as a hedge in their investment algorithms because of the fixed rates of exchange between the international currencies.

So what might the implementation of such a system of paperless, credit card-less currencies look like in poor countries and in developed countries? And what would prevent fraud such as people signing up more than once and receiving more than one monthly stipend and/or stealing money from other people by forcing them to make purchases on their behalf by gunpoint?

The system might look something like the following:

1. Small groups or cells would be established of say 20 to 30 people and one or more people could be paid extra Dots to serve as the "Dot Master" for that group for any period of time. A Dot Master

would need to be on duty for each group 24 hours per day 7 days per week so there may be more than one Dot Master per group working in shifts.

2. The Dot master would be in charge of keeping records of everyone in their group and how many Dots they should have on account. Each month the Dot master would credit their account with their monthly supply of Dots. More importantly every time someone wanted to buy something the transaction would have to be cleared by the Dot Master who would debt the customer's record of account and credit the vendors account (manually on paper in areas where there are no phones and computers). The additional responsibilities of the Dot Master and members of the group would be to make sure that no-one is abusing the system by creating fictitious persona's taking double payments, or using someone-else's Dot account without their permission, etc..

3. On a periodic basis the Dot masters would then report the balance sheet of their entire group to an up-line of other Dot Masters who maintain records for 20 to 30 Dot Masters below them. The levels of this up line (or the total number of down lines) can expand and contract as needed without limitation using a similar structure as a binary search tree. By reporting to the up-line Dot Masters records are not only backed up but reports can be made of members of the Dot group who may be traveling and who may need to purchase goods, services, food, lodging and transportation services from other groups at a distance. In addition, Dot Masters at higher levels could help to prevent abuse of the system at lower levels.

The system is that simple. Records can be kept both electronically as well as on paper thus diminishing the need for any dependency on technology and lowering the risks associated with computer hackers.

I have found that even in the most remote war torn countries of Africa and other countries cell phone service is available and more people than you might expect have cell phones. Cell phones would not be required but would make things convenient for those in the most remote areas and those who do not use high technology. None-the-less, if you think of the system now with Dot Masters that do have cell phones and who utilize revolving code words throughout their network of Dot Masters then you have a payment system network that does not require the use of any hard currency or any plastic credit cards or anything other than use of hand written records. The validation of peoples identity could even be conducted by a simple call from one Dot Master to the member's Dot Master in real time and the people could all be put in contact with each other instantly to ensure no fraudulent transactions take place.

As with any system there are potential situations where fraud can occur but the records kept are simple enough to also back up on paper and Dots can easily be re-allocated to victims and stripped from offenders. Any kind of fraud in the Dot system that did occur would not threaten the value of Dots or have the potential to destroy the entire system (unlike the monetary systems we have in place today). Thus the Dot system is superior to and much safer, more reliable and more flexible than our current monetary and payment systems.

However for the sake of discussion let's identify potential security vulnerabilities in the system.

The Dot system could be vulnerable to phone taps and computer hacking if and when phones are used. A distributed network of software and computers will most likely be used in the higher levels of the up-line to facilitate the global system even though the entire system could be done by hand. In order to help correct and prevent any fraud that may arise as a result of computer hackers hard copies of records on paper will still be accessible to Dot Masters (and used exclusively in areas where phones and or computers are unavailable).

Using this Dot system there would be no way to prevent war lords or others from pointing a gun at someone and forcing them to spend their Dots for the benefit of the criminal with the gun. However, at least in this system the person who is "robbed" can report the robbery and can have their supply of stolen Dots replaced with the stroke of a pen. Criminals and other despots when caught could be tried and jailed and/or they can have their supply of Dots restricted or debited as punishment.

Everyone in the Dot system would easily and almost instantaneously be able to vote entire groups of people out of the Dot system, like despots and their subordinates, as punishment for their activities. Similarly, users of the Dot system could vote to restrict the sale of weapons by allowing people to spend their Dots on weapons but by not allowing the receiver of the Dots to spend those Dots on anything. Dots can be regulated at the higher echelons of the Dot Master hierarchy in such a way as to keep people who break the laws of the Dot currency from using their Dots anywhere or at least anywhere outside of their own Dot group of 20 to 30 people.

I was going to make a really good fiction novel and movie screen play involving the creation of a system like the Dot system in Africa in order to show how that continent could become the terminators of poverty. I imagined the story line would have interesting fictional characters like greedy international bankers and businessmen who get blindsided by the introduction of this Dot system that ends poverty in Africa. I might still write the book and movie, but I believe now that my characters really will be fictional because, as I've pointed out, I don't know that there would be anyone who would oppose such a new currency. The advent of a new currency such as the Dot that is issued to everyone each month would only create more consumers and more business and more profit for everyone concerned and would take nothing away from existing currencies and would in fact add stability to existing currencies that they lack today.

Unbeknownst to me in 2007 when I thought of the Dot there were already new virtual currencies being successfully implemented online. One such virtual currency is the BitCoin, which is now a very popular currency that is even traded at retail currency trading firms against the currencies of other countries and gold. BitCoins can be purchased online from dozens of global currency exchange houses both regulated and unregulated.

You can't hold BitCoins in your hand but BitCoins can be used to buy goods and services online just like any other currency and can also be converted back into any other currency in a matter of minutes. One of the biggest reasons why BitCoins have become so popular is the perception by the general public that spending of BitCoins can be done anonymously and stored anonymously and can thus be used to hide money and financial transactions. However, as an electrical and computer engineer I can think of dozens of ways for the law enforcement or intelligence agencies to find those people who make use of BitCoins by simply keeping track of where the money is being converted back and forth into conventional bankable currencies. My own opinion is simply that while some transactions in BitCoins may be untraceable, there will still be ways to catch those people who the government really wants to find that use Bitcoins via the points of conversion and thus this idea of this privacy may be not be as valuable as people think.

Nonetheless, the fact that BitCoins have come into existence is fantastic and its use and evolution proves that new currencies can be created by people at will and valued by the will of the people who use them. The creators of BitCoin did not create the currency with the same goals in mind as I have and thus the BitCoin currency still fluctuates on an open market with other currencies of the world and the only way to obtain BitCoins is to either purchase them or 'mine' for them using powerful networks of computers in an increasingly costly way much in the same manner as one would mine for gold in the frozen waters of the Bering Sea.

But now that BitCoins exist and the model of a virtual currency has been proven we can now create a new virtual currency (let's call it the "Dot") using the same technology in order to bring into existence the very things that we outlined in previous chapters including:

1. Creating currency exchange rate boundaries between all international currencies by simply creating the upper and lower exchange rate values of our new currency the Dot or by simply fixing the value to specific exchange rates.

2. Provide for immediate transactions using Dots, just like BitCoins.

3. Instead of forcing people to mine for BitCoins simply issue users of Dots a monthly stipend that even pays for their taxes and medical insurance in their own countries.   Anyone caught exchanging Dots outside of their prescribed exchange rate boundaries could lose their rights to receive a monthly stipend or even use the system (this feature may be unnecessary).

4. Use the same infrastructure and methods as BitCoin to enable people to buy Dots using their existing currencies and to convert back to their existing currencies from Dots.

5. Provide the means for additional payments of Dots to be made to the tax collecting authorities of the various countries on behalf of those who receive Dot stipends in order to pay the tax bill for the Dots that they are given (or that they purchase).

Other components of the plan that could be considered include:

a. Inviting governments to receive some stipends

to pay for some of their expenses and incorporate use of the Dot currency in their own systems or in some cases to even switch to the Dot completely. I am not in favor of completely eliminating the national currencies of other countries, because I view this as partial loss of their sovereignty and there still needs to be alternatives for people who become excluded from using Dots or do not wish to use Dots. The objective of the Dot system is not world dominance but rather assistance for the citizens and peaceful governments of the world.

b. A way of revoking or lowering the monthly stipend for people whose governments also start providing a stipend of their own. The idea isn't designed to make people rich but provide for a basic standard of living.

c. Using Dot's to buy life insurance policies that pay Dot's back or implement a system I call, "The Rollback". The Rollback would be a monthly % charge that would be debited from everyone's account proportionally in order to remove an equal number of Dot's from the system as have been paid out to those people who have died that month. By using the Rollback payment system there would be no need to use life insurance policies as a means to keep the money supply bound by the number of people that use it.

The only thing that would need to take place in order to create this new Dot currency would be for enough people and businesses to want to implement the features described above. People who would like to help usher in these monthly stipends would simply need to start accepting and using Dots as payments for goods and services, just as people have started using BitCoins. I've already identified currency speculators and those in economically depressed countries as having means and motivations to utilize the Dot system so I can see an immediate attraction for its implementation.

The software to mimic the security of BitCoins is already available because BitCoin is an open source software system. There would need to be some revisions in the BitCoin software made in order to facilitate the Dot Masters and the distribution of Dots because the Dot system does have differences with BitCoin system particularly in how Dots can be obtained. There are some people smarter than myself and major businesses that have taken my advice and are already working on an implementation of the Dot Money system (for more information see www.DotMoneyBook.com).

Ideally we would also create the infrastructure of the Dot Masters to overlay onto or insert into the system so that it could be also be used by people who don't have computers and who may only have cell phones or even no phones at all. If the currency takes off we could pay to provide Dot Masters in underdeveloped countries with cell phones or other means of communication necessary for them to participate in the Dot system and receive monthly stipends themselves. We are talking about a limitless borderless implementation of a new currency that would provide all users with minimum living benefit, that could replace stolen money, and where all users of the currency could vote on such things as:

a. what would be considered prohibited transactions and;
b. what the process would look like that would initiate a vote by all users of the system in

order to exclude groups or individuals from use of the system;

c. methods to sanction certain users and transactions (i.e. the sale of arms, theft and fraud, etc.).

A very useful feature of the system is that money stolen could automatically be replaced.

The method of establishing a new virtual currency like the Dot may end up being the fastest way to achieve all of the goals of this book without the need for politicians to change any law of any country. This may be the way for ordinary people to establish international currency rate boundaries, end poverty, provide for the cost of medical expenses and pay everyone's income taxes. All that we would need to create this currency is the will to use it. Imagine how effective this system would be if one or more governments joined in to supported use of the Dot. If countries such as the United States, Canada, United Kingdom, Germany, France, Australia, China or any other powerful countries did so this would help to accelerate the process of implementation.

Chapter 17: Who Is Against the U.S. Dollar

I am hard pressed to find any good reason for any country to object to the U.S. implementing such a new monetary system. Even if there were powerful countries that objected then what would it profit them to intentionally devalue the U.S. dollar? What would be in it for them? How would they go about banning the exchange of the U.S. dollar from the businesses that depend on the exchange of their currency with the U.S. dollar in order to survive? Is there any major country that would not be negatively affected by a devaluation of the U.S. dollar?

As far as I can see there would be nothing to gain by any country in the world who tried to engage in economic warfare against the United States. Particularly if you consider that such economic warfare could lead to military action. If the standard of living of the people in the U.S. or any other major country were sufficiently threatened then war may ensue to cure economic differences. Who would risk this and why? I think it would be much more likely that the other large countries of the world would change their systems according to our model and seek membership, with the U.S., in an international association that establishes currency rate boundaries.

People who argue that China would take us to war over the debt that we owe them wouldn't have much to argue about because China would immediately be paid the debt owed it plus interest in brand new U.S. dollars. Also consider the fact that our country is such an important trade partner to China that the Chinese already engage in and depend heavily on fixing currency rates between the Chinese currency and the U.S. dollar. Technically China is ahead of the curve in its policies of fixing currency rates and attempting to broker deals with other countries to do the same.

I believe that the Chinese government already fully understands the value in establishing fixed boundaries on the rates of currency exchange. I believe China sees "the writing on the wall" in regards to our perilous practice of allowing currency rates to fluctuate without boundaries. Of course China, like any other country, has its problems and this book is not a debate on the merits of the Chinese government compared to any other. Rather this book is about sound monetary practice. In regards to monetary practice it appears to me that the Chinese already acknowledge the abstract nature of the value of money and they are more likely to use money as a tool to sustain global stability rather than allow money to destroy it.

Chapter 18: Who Agrees About Fiat Money

The fact that the major nations of the world print fiat money is not in dispute by any notable authorities. A very short list of those who agree that currency exchanges rates should be bound includes many members of the U.S. Federal Reserve, such as Arthur J. Rolnick, the Senior Vice President and Director of Research (1985-2010) and Warren E. Weber who is a retired economist. Former Fed chief Paul Volcker recently called for "the need to develop an international monetary system worthy of our time." Steve Forbes author of the book "Money" appears to also romanticize about the days of fixed currency rates afforded by the Bretton Woods Accord, and he also endorses a practical method of fixing currency exchange rates to gold in order to help achieve better economic results.

The list of people who advocate that a stipend should be paid to people to allow people to maintain at least some minimum standard of living may surprise you. The list includes, Milton Friedman who called it the Negative Income Tax. Even conservative political leaders like Charles Murray believe that redistribution under our existing systems via direct cash payments would result in $1 trillion less than of the cost of the current system when phased in over 10 years. Murray estimates a $10,000 flat cash payment per year would suffice; while I believe a Net benefits package of about $19,000 per year would be better after health care, state and federal taxes and life insurance were also factored.

Many people are surprised to find that there is support for one form or another of a basic income among both historical classical liberals, such as Adam Smith and John Stuart Mill, as well as more recent thinkers such as Friedrich Hayek and Milton Friedman. Hayek, for example, wrote this passage in his book Law, Legislation, and Liberty:

"The assurance of a certain minimum income for everyone, or a sort of floor below which nobody need fall even when he is unable to provide for himself, appears not only to be a wholly legitimate protection against a risk common to all, but a necessary part of the Great Society in which the individual no longer has specific claims on the members of the particular small group into which he was born."

Many libertarians are also in favor of a minimum monthly income to replace the current welfare systems. Matt Zwolinski is an Associate Professor of Philosophy at the University of San Diego, and the founder of, and frequent contributor to, the Bleeding Heart Libertarians. As Zwolinski puts it in an essay on the subject, classical liberals adhere to *"the principle that a society's legal rules and/or moral principles must be justified to each and every individual who is subject to them, and that such justification requires demonstrating that those rules or principles are ones that each individual has reason to support."*

In his article A Universal Basic Income: Conservative, Progressive, and Libertarian Perspectives (Part 3 of a Series) author Ed Dolan states, *"Many classical liberals think that, given the choice, freedom-loving individuals would prefer to live in a system where the minimal state, in addition to protecting people and their property from criminals and foreign enemies, had some mechanism for providing everyone with a minimum income to fall back on in case of misfortune."*

Writing for Reason.com, Matthew Feeney puts it this way:

"[L]ibertarians in the U.S. and elsewhere should support the idea of a basic income as a replacement for the current welfare systems on offer. The welfare system in the U.S. is an ineffective and expensive mess, but it is unlikely that the majority of the American public are going to be persuaded to support the outright abolition of the welfare state any time soon. Rather than make the principled argument against the redistribution of wealth, libertarians would do better if they were to argue for a welfare system that promotes personal responsibility, reduces the humiliation."

Finally, one of the most inspiring calls for the institution of the basic income came recently in Switzerland.   Under Swiss law, citizens can organize popular initiatives that result in direct political action. The country usually holds several referenda a year.   What some considered a publicity stunt at first eventually lead to enough petitions being signed to vote on a basic income of $2,800 being considered by the government of

Switzerland. The so-called 1:12 initiative was voted on by the people of Switzerland in November of 2013. Roughly 65% of Swiss voters opposed the 1:12 Initiative for Fair Pay, according to results from all of the country's 26 cantons reported by Swiss television. Another 34% supported the proposal. I believe that there are two reasons why the initiative failed. The first reason is because of the potential increase in taxes would need to be raised in the long term to pay everyone. Few people like the idea of putting more tax burden on earners. The second reason that I believe the initiative failed was because it was named for the organizers' belief that no one in a Swiss company should earn more in a month than someone else makes in a year. There are very few people who support ideas that involve forced redistribution of wealth and fewer people that believe that it is fair to cap the earning potential of anyone. I believe that if there would have been no increase in taxes and if there were no limitation placed on earnings of individuals as is the case in my plan then this basic income measure would have passed in Switzerland.

While I do not advocate the capping of anyone's salaries, taking from the rich to give to the poor, use of any income tax or any other means to impose financial equality to citizens of any country, I am in favor of paying everyone a basic income and I do believe that the time is near when this will become a reality for the good of everyone. To me this vote in Switzerland is evidence many people are beginning to see the light. My examination of monetary policies show that the minimum income could be supplied at no cost to anyone. If this is not reason enough to take action I don't know what is.

Finally, aside from Libertarians, I don't see any conflict of interest for political parties on the left or the right. In fact, I see a solution that can accommodate the major grievances of all major political parties. On one side you have the ability to end the income tax system and on the other side you have the ability to provide for the poor and needy and to elevate them to a basic standard of living. Capitalists could keep their profits and the wealthy could remain wealthy and have even more consumers with money to buy their goods and services. At the same time unskilled laborers or those people who are not interested in going to college, could chose to focus on whatever they most love. Using my system anyone could take even the lowest paying jobs and still live with dignity and do better than just making ends meet. People would truly be free to pursue what makes them happy which would result in a more vibrant an healthy society that provides higher quality of service because people are doing jobs they chose to do rather than jobs they are forced to do.

Chapter 19: A Matter Of National Security

Issues that threaten the security of the government or our ways of life are often deemed to be issues of National Security. Depending on the severity of the underlying issues matters of National Security are often treated with such extreme measures that the term National Security is frequently used to justify secret, unilateral action by government officials, which may include the breaking of the laws of the country. National Security is normally thought of as a reason to take extraordinary measures to ensure that the government and its citizens survive and persist to as strong a degree as possible no matter what circumstances arise.

Governments, politicians, officials and citizens who are concerned about issues of National Security that threaten the condition of their country are strongly urged to adopt the monetary policies that I have provided in this book in order reduce the risks associated with the current lack of bounded exchange rates. In addition, the current monetary policies that create unnecessary budget deficits also expose us to potentially negative and unpredictable global economic impacts. By the use of various social welfare programs the majority of governments around the world appear to recognize the importance of providing 'the poor' with the ability to sustain themselves. I believe that even the rich and middle class would rather see poor people taken care of then trip over the poor on every street corner.

At the same time many governments also appear to recognize that the practice of taxation is increasingly discouraging entrepreneurs from staying in their home countries and is instead leading to a redistribution of wealth on a global scale as many wealthy people move to countries with tax advantages and end up spending their money there.

The entire practice of imposing an income tax is becoming an unwieldy process of forcing business owners to track the financial practices of their customers and report them to various governments around the world which in turn stifles the flow of money throughout the entire economy. The complexity of these reporting systems has become a "beast" in itself that provides no benefit to consumers and discourages the transmission of capital by businesses. As the failing systems of income tax become more complex and onerous they result in ever increasing imposition of government social controls that interfere with the everyday life of citizens. In the United States you are no longer able to protect yourself from potential prison sentences for failing to fill in your tax returns properly even if you hire a certified accountant do it for you. If an accountant makes a mistake, you still may face criminal prosecution at the discretion of one or more attorneys at the U.S. Department of Justice who may have time on their hands. The entire concept of forcibly taking from the rich to give to the poor or to take from the middle class to support government expenditures that are essentially controlled by the rich creates an ongoing disenchantment that discourages patriotism.

Even more pressing are a host of unknowns that can throw any of the developed nations into chaos and cause their currencies to become worthless overnight. In the United States there are laws that allow the government to issue more currency in times of national emergencies. However, that is not enough because, if a country is under such extreme duress that it is required to purchase assistance from outside of its boarders then it would be essential to have a currency that does not diminish in value when exchanged for other global currencies.

Presently, the lack of international exchange rate controls leaves all of the developed countries exposed to a variety of threats to their National Security. Below I have provided a short list of potential threats to the U.S. for which our current monetary system is inadequate. The events are so catastrophic as to require help from other countries if they were not equally incapacitated. This same list of threats can be applied to any developed nation since all capitalist, socialist and remaining communist countries all use the same antiquated monetary systems. As you read the following list of threats, think about how much easier it would be for any country to recover from the threats if everyone were already receiving a monthly stipend:

- Terrorist attacks (including use of fire arms, explosives, nuclear, chemical or biological agents on our home land)
- Internet attacks (including disabling online infrastructure of banks and e-commerce)
- Acts of war (including acts of war perpetrated against our country or NATO allies and nuclear war that happens between other countries like Pakistan and India, Iran and Israel, or North Korea)
- Outbreak of disease (including diseases similar to Ebola, Small Pox, Enterovirus, Bird Flu, etc.)
- Climate change that causes slow or rapidly occurring weather events that render areas uninhabitable or inaccessible (i.e. severe and lasting winter storms, hurricanes, tornados, heat waves, floods, etc.)
- Solar Flares (disabling global power grids, land and sea vehicles and other modes of transportation making the delivery of food impossible)
- Meteor (a large enough meteor that strikes a country could leave it completely devastated)
- Nuclear Power Plant Disaster (including unforeseen design flaws that are exploited by terrorists or that occur due to unforeseen

natural disasters like those that were not forecast by the designers of the Fukushima nuclear power plant in Japan)

- Depression or Recession of the Economy (as and when the more frequent and inevitable bubbles occur under our current economic Ponzi scheme the results become less predictable)
- Depression or Recession of a Foreign Economy (something people often overlook is what would happen to the U.S. economy if any of our stronger allies or trade partners economy collapsed for any reason listed, including China)
- The Continued Increase in the National Debt (this can lead to rapid and unknown currency rate devaluations and failures of critical infrastructure including operation of the government, the military and the payments of critical programs like social security, and the benefits of other welfare recipients)
- Discontent of the poor (including more severe protests from groups such as 'Occupy Wall Street' or protests such as in Ferguson Missouri)
- Negative interactions with extraterrestrial beings.
- Panic over any of the events described above.

The list above contains known threats to the National Security of the United States that can also be applied to other developed nations. There are undoubtedly more threats than those listed above. If we fail to plan for any of these events today, then we are leaving the future of our country and our National Security to chance. Currently, as things stand, given that there are solutions as described in this book, I believe that our politicians and our citizens would be irresponsible if they did not adopt a new monetary system that would increase our ability to survive potential disasters. The implementation of the monetary systems described in this book would at least give us the best possible odds to survive any of the above events, by empowering the government with enough money necessary to apply to the problems and enabling our country to purchase help from outside if necessary. The monthly stipend for the citizens of the country would give them a better chance of surviving life changing events and they would be better equipped to assist those in need without having to worry about their own needs. The infrastructure to provide additional monetary payments to people who suffered from any of the above disasters would already be in place.

Chapter 20: How The World Would Be Better

Imagine a world that implemented the monetary policies that I suggest. Below is a short list of some of the potential problems that face us that could be solved (obviously the same benefits would be available to other countries).

- Homelessness and poverty would be eliminated, yet people would still be able to accumulate and keep wealth if they so desired.

- The money supply of the country would expand and shrink as needed based on the population of each country.

- There would always be enough people with enough money to spend to keep the economy healthy even in times of disaster, recession or depression.

- The country would be better prepared to withstand disasters and threats to National Security.

- The image of our governments and politicians would be improved amongst citizens.

- Everyone would have the medical care that they need.

- There would be money available to people to go to public or private schools and to attend higher education and Universities. Government would have the money to also put back into state Universities and primary schools improving education for everyone without worry about cost.

- There would no longer be any need for the government to borrow money and existing debts of the government could be immediately repaid with interest.

- The individual income tax systems as well as corporate tax systems could be eliminated completely, along with the albatross of global reporting requirements that is stifling growth.

- There would be no reason to eliminate any existing government or private sector jobs or infrastructure. Those who work for the IRS could be transferred to the Social Security Administration to help with benefit payments.

- There would be no need for financial institutions to maintain the vast, expensive and cumbersome surveillance on their customers and reporting apparatus that sends information to the multitude of different tax authorities for tax purposes. The reporting infrastructure could be reduced to surveillance only for the sake of law enforcement.

- Individuals would be able to pick and choose their careers and jobs rather than being forced to spend the bulk of their time and energy working at jobs that they do not like barely making ends meet. Parents would have more flexibility in only taking part time jobs so that they could spend more time with their families if they liked. In theory, because people would be working at jobs by choice, customers would receive a higher standard of service from happy workers.

- Funds would be available to make sure that children were well cared for with their needs being met.

- Although the government would have the money to continue to offer and maintain public schools, individuals would have funds to go to private schools if they wished and they would have the money to attend university or pay to obtain other career training.

- The government would have the money to insure and replace money lost as a result of fraud in government regulated businesses like the stock market or to help compensate victims of other crimes.

- Many of the social programs could be eliminated and replaced with one monthly cash payment to citizens.

- People would be happier in general because they would not have to worry as much about money.

- Businesses would be incentivized to hire people from their own countries because the citizens pay would already be subsidized by the monthly stipend from the government and thus many jobs that now pay high salaries could be reduced (as long as not below two thirds of the existing minimum wage).

- Immigration could be simplified as non-citizens (the so called non-documented workers) could be allowed to remain in the country as long as they had jobs and a place to live, but they would need to be paid at least minimum wage and would need their healthcare to be paid for by the employer. Again, this would inspire citizens to hire people from their own country rather than foreigners because the minimum wage for stipend earners could be reduced to two thirds of the legal requirement and it would reduce the need to deport non-citizens or exclude them from geographic territories. Let foreigners stay, but let it be a crime to pay them anything less than the full minimum wage and pay for their medical benefits.

- The government would have the money to begin to actually offer services that further help stimulate the economy and business. The government could offer things like, environmental clean-up services at no cost to the businesses. This would help provide for a cleaner, safer environment while at the same time allowing companies to make new products and make money without having to spend on clean up. Companies would now be encouraged to disclose the chemicals that they are using so that they could be properly cleaned up by the government at no cost. The infrastructure provided by the government for such services would add value (create capital) itself that backs and justifies the issuance of the currency required just as shares of public companies are valued based on their infrastructure and capacity to provide services. Countries would actually be inspired and able to compete against each other in providing services like environmental clean up to support business growth and production to attract and build new business in their countries.

- There would be money available to pay military, law enforcement, teachers and other public servants much better wages and provide for their incentives.

- There would be money to help rehabilitate criminals rather than just throw them into prison to rot.

- Funds would be available to help recover from disasters.

- Crime would decrease as fewer people would need to steal in order to survive.

- New inventions in science, philosophy, art and music would be made as a result of the time available to people that would allow them to experiment and pursue happiness.

- Republicans and Democrats would have fewer things to argue about.

There are many more benefits that would result from implementing the monetary policies in this book.

Chapter 21: Potential Problems of the System

The solutions in this book are certainly not a panacea that will make everything better and solve all of the problems of the world. It is the lot of human beings to experience hardships as well as good times. For every disease that we cure another one seems to arise to take its place. For every enemy that we destroy a new one presents itself. For every problem that is solved another crops up.

People hope that science, technology, philosophy and spirituality will make the experience of life as comfortable as possible for everyone. Thus I argue that we should leverage our existing technology and our understanding, experience and use of money in order to help streamline and improve the experience of life for as many as possible. However, I can easily see a multitude of new problems that may arise as we move to this new system, none of which are insurmountable.

Below is a short list of some problems that I foresee that may or may not arise as a result of the implementation of the new monetary systems that include the monthly stipend. My point is not to prevent us from implementing the new system because of insurmountable potential problems, but to simply be aware and prepare ourselves to deal with these potentialities.

- Many more people will have money to purchase items that require natural resources to produce, such as cell phones and computer equipment. Thus an additional strain on the environment may occur as a result of the increase in consumption and disposal of natural resources associated with many products. There would also be more money available to fix these problems and create new businesses or government agencies that actively perform environmental cleaning and stabilization.

- Temporary price controls may need to be implemented as a result of spikes in the increase demand for certain products. In some cases permanent price controls may need to be applied to certain commodities. Temporary hyper inflation could be controlled by starting with lower monthly payments and increasing the payments over time until they reach their targets.

- Treaties and standards to place caps on military spending and on monthly stipend payments will need to be worked out between countries that utilize these monetary policies so as not to create extreme imbalances of standards of living. Such treaties and spending caps could likely be facilitated through participation in currency rate boundary associations.

- It is possible that several currency rate boundary associations may arise that compete with each other based on political ideology and it is unclear how this would impact world peace. It is likely that member nations of NATO would constitute one group and it is also likely that China (and Russia) would participate directly or indirectly (by continuing to fix their currency rates of exchange on the USD).

- Terrorists and other troublemakers could conceivably gain access to more capital to fund their efforts; however, there would also be larger budgets available to counter their activities.

- Addictions from alcohol and drugs may increase; however, there would be unlimited money available to provide addiction deterrence and treatment.

I do not find that any of the problems listed in this section are unsolvable or big enough to make implementation of the system unattractive. Leaving the current system in place is liable to do far more damage than implementing the new system even if it comes with the problems discussed in this section.

Chapter 22: In Defense of Welfare

I am not a fan of our welfare system in its current manifestation that takes by force from the rich and middle class and redistributes to the poor. However, I acknowledge that a system of social welfare of some kind must exist in order for the wealthy and middle class to also enjoy the fruits of their labors uninterrupted by the needs of others.

I have firsthand experience with the welfare system as my family and I have had to utilize it ourselves because of unforeseen events and I am not ashamed for taking the aid. Based on my experience some of the staunchest detractors of welfare are the first in line to receive benefits when they become needy for whatever reason. I have included this chapter because I get tired of listening to the irrational arguments of those that oppose welfare even in its broken condition. My hope is to address the most foolish and popular perceptions and put them to rest once and for all.

Too often when we ask ourselves how we can help the poor we presuppose that we are above the poor. We act like they are the poor and we will not be poor because of who we are. Anyone, no matter how wealthy, can lose everything through no fault of their own. We also fail to see that the existence of the poor in the first place is a sign of our own poverty because we cannot sufficiently provide for those who are in need or, conversely, completely eliminate poverty. Thus, the very fact that the poor exist is a testimony to the fact that we are all poor by association. Considering the fact that any one of us, no matter how powerful, can fall into poverty we should ask ourselves what we would like our potential poverty to look like. I find that many people are simply unable or unwilling to think about what circumstances might occur in their own lives that could result in their descent into poverty. We are all connected to each other and allowing some people to exist in poverty will ultimately lead to negative consequences for those who are not.

In my opinion the biggest potential threat to our global economy and the human race is our failure to really care for those who are less fortunate. I give kudos to those who try to uplift the poor and help others who are less fortunate. However, we are not doing enough to guarantee the survival of the human race. Even within developed counties we still don't quite get the necessity for many social programs and many try hard to limit welfare benefits even though denying these benefits to those who need them, for whatever reason, will only hurt us all in the end.

Obviously, according to the principals in this book, I don't believe that, in order to help the poor, we need to forcibly take from the wealthy or discourage people from accumulating wealth. But no matter what system we use to uplift the poor we have to acknowledge that our entire society is only as strong as its weakest link and financially speaking there are a lot of weak links.

Current popular thinking is that we want all want a society where everyone is well educated and happy to work for every dime that they make and willing to hand money over, through taxes and donations, for the greater good of everyone else. Doing good work is an admirable virtue that is healthy for human beings and without which most people decay rather than evolve. However, there is a fallacy in our current popular opinion the dictates that work must be hard in order for success to be appreciated. How hard and undesirable does work have to be and what about those people who really enjoy their work? Should work supersede all other functions of our lives? What about those people who are born into wealth or who have to do very little work if any at all because they have achieved some kind of "success?"

I have no issue with measuring the quality of peoples work, but why can't we work on things that we do enjoy? Why must we work 40 hours per week instead of 20? Who makes these rules?

Henry David Thoreau the author of Walden Pond, observed that he only really needed to work for about 3 months out of the year in order to grow enough food on which to live comfortably. However, because we have adopted this system of property division the majority of us are born into a system that keeps us working a minimum of 40 hours per week (usually much more) and remain unable to make ends meet even if we have graduated from a university. For most of us, the privilege of just getting by requires us to find a way to go to college and study in some field where jobs are available rather than study something that we really like. We are made to believe that we should feel happy about these circumstances. The advent of computers that were supposed to do work for us and save our time have actually lengthened our work days and made it possible for us to work in every location at all times. All these ideas are forced upon us at the same time that parents are chastised about not spending enough time with their children usually because they have to work. Many parents are forced to outsource the entire upbringing of their children by paying others to care for them while the parents work just to make enough money to survive. When children break down and commit acts of violence we then blame the parents for not being involved in the lives of their children.

Now consider life from the perspective of someone born in a country like The Democratic Republic of the Congo or Liberia or Zimbabwe where the standard of living and economic conditions are among the lowest in the world. As residents in first world countries, why should we care? In fact, some would say, it is Gods will that some are born into poverty and we are just lucky that we were born here. Yet, God gave us all free will. So the real question is why don't we (those in the developed countries) do more to help the poor in other countries?

The answers to that question are complex. If I had to guess I would say one practical reason is because we are so busy just trying to maintain our own standard of living that we don't have a lot of time and resources available to really do much to help others. Another reason is because of our own lack of political will to take action to help others. As a race we have not yet began to connect the dots between ourselves and people who are impoverished on the other side of the world or even on our own continent. We are taught that people are poor because they don't work or that they don't have a good education, but we do little to create jobs or to provide education. We look at the issue as "their problem" and fail to see how it eventually inhibits us until we are impacted by disease, war, crime and illegal border crossings. We just want to secure our boarders and keep the problems and the undesirables outside of our own country. We send insufficient aid in part because the global monetary system is too cumbersome and unstable to enable us to send more and adequate financial aid.

Even in our own country there is a constant battle between those who want to expand social welfare and those who want to end welfare programs altogether, even if doing so would send levels of crime soaring and even if it means an endless stream of people living in the streets. It's much easier for an educated and employed person who had luck in their favor to simply say to the poor, "well why don't you just do like I did, go to college and work really hard and then..." In many cases, we are asking some people to do something that is impossible. In many cases we are asking people to do something that we would be unable to achieve ourselves given the same circumstances of the people who we advise. In many cases simply providing a road map for people is the same thing as saying, "go be lucky." It's not enough.

The very things we are asking of many people is to essentially solve their own problems and change their own economic conditions with as little help from us as possible while we refuse to acknowledge the help that we have received. I'm not saying this is true for all cases, but I'm saying that it is true to the extent that all of our well intentioned advice hereto has not ended poverty.

Even people who are willing to work hard and take full responsibility for themselves and their future cannot overcome the problem of lack of money in supply that leads to lack of adequate paying jobs.

When it comes to the poor in other countries, we think of the problem as resting with their country and their government and so we simply to take too little action. We take action only when a country such as Liberia is overrun with the Ebola virus and we feel threatened by their inability, in their poverty, to deal with such a deadly and contagious virus. Only when rogue organizations in Africa and the Middle East start kidnapping, raping and enslaving women and children, and beheading American and British journalists do we start to see how factors such as their lack of education possibly inhibits them from being able to read and understand their own religious texts. Only then do we see how, *inter alia*, lack of education in other parts of the world ends up directly affecting us. To further my point simply look at the education levels of our most feared enemies of the developed nations in the world.

The fact of the matter is that there is no way to maintain peace and stability in the first world countries when in the rest of the world the majority of people lack access to suitable education, medicine, food and shelter. It's like a classic science fiction movie where the elite live in an isolated utopia that is destined to be overrun by the sheer numbers and masses of poor people. In the real world no matter how good our intentions are, we often make matters worse when we are forced to intervene militarily in countries with half hearted resolve, and where we unwittingly create new enemies out of generations of uneducated and misunderstood people whose relatives we've killed in combat. I'm not suggesting that these are our intentions, however, history has shown that our own weapons end up being used against us whenever we prematurely depart from territory that we have conquered through battle. Often we leave because of monetary constraints before securing the hearts minds and future of those that we have conquered, which causes the cycle of violence to repeat. There can be no democracy amongst generations of people that we have not yet taken the time to care for through lengthy and expensive education.

While I see no sin in being financially wealthy, I would go as far as to say that the problems experienced by the people of these poor countries is the responsibility of every person on earth and every developed nation that governs over them by force and necessity. The problems that arise in these impoverished countries that do eventually make their way into our media and affect our lives are a direct result of our own selfishness nature and foolishness by some in believing that we are not connected with these people when in reality we are all interconnected and interdependent. These people, the poor and the rich, the under educated and the educated, the sick and the healthy, they are all our brothers and sisters and what hurts them will eventually hurt us and what they do will eventually have a direct impact on our lives. This is why we must care for each other not just in our hearts and minds but in our deeds (even whether we like to care or not). Anyone who wants to maintain the quality of their own lifestyle must work to help others to develop theirs or risk losing it all.

Under the current conditions that we impose upon ourselves through government and failed monetary systems I have no choice but to be in favor of social welfare. I see the obvious need for it. As I said I am not for the type of welfare that takes from the rich by force through taxes in order to make everyone equal, or redistribute wealth. Rather, I propose solutions that suggest that nothing need be taken from anyone and our current unworkable system has never really been necessary in the first place. I am for everyone being properly compensated for the use of the property of the world that they would be able to access freely if it were not for the constructs of our global systems of government and property ownership.

One of the biggest arguments against welfare is that recipients will become lethargic and uninspired to rise above their own circumstances. The argument goes that we must not give enough welfare for people to be comfortable particularly when the money is being taken (begrudgingly) from the rest of us. The argument is that if we make people comfortable on welfare then they will not want to get off and others will want to sign up.

These arguments all presuppose that people are just lazy. They fail to take into consideration the rate of expansion and contraction of the population that is poor. It's like arguing that all of the people who are affected by recession should be helped out in a way that keeps them from being comfortable. If this thinking were true then it would stand to reason that those who inherit fortunes and those whose parents are wealthy should also be kept from living comfortable lives unless they prove their worth. Remember the same arguments that you use against the nature of the poor can also be made against the rich.

Many of the wealthiest people in the world have all had help from someone or some group in order to enable them to achieve greater wealth. This help that they received, be it from family, investors or from a government program, still constitutes welfare. Anyone that has enough provision to spend time doing something that they enjoy is faring well. People who make arguments about the nature of poor people do not see that every person who lives in a developed nation has benefited from welfare throughout their lives. Everyone born into a developed nation has had things prepared for them since before they were born or able to pay for any of them. During their lives they have been given many things for which they themselves have not had to pay. The only question is the degree to which we will allow people to receive more. Whether you were born into wealth or poverty, if you were born into a developed nation then you have benefited from, been the recipient of and made use of social welfare either directly or indirectly. I have provided a list in Appendix D of some of the social welfare benefits that people in developed countries have at their disposal and it is indisputable that both the rich and poor have all benefited from the things in this list.

I have shown evidence that because of the lack of money in the system it is not possible to eliminate poverty nor is it possible to even sustain a high enough ratio of people who live in the middle class because there is simply not enough money to capitalize the comfortable existence of the population. Thus, under the current monetary system, there will always be a higher number of poor people or ones who are unable to achieve a basic standard of living, and the ratio of poor people is destined to grow. There is no magical formula of social welfare benefits to be distributed that will result in fewer recipients because the current economic system ensures an increasing need for benefits. So you can no longer blame everyone who is poor because they fail to try harder. In the long run the best that any poor person can do is to simply displace someone from a higher income class. Those who continue to defend the current system continue to condemn us all to a world where poverty exists unnecessarily. Those who continue to defend the current system engage in what is known as "System Justification" which really just gets in the way of new solutions. Historically speaking there has always been a steady percentage of people living in poverty. The only difference between today and the past is that by giving people food stamps they do not starve to death. By supplying free education crime is reduced. And by supplying free medical care (whatever the standard) more poor people are able to sustain their lives rather than contracting and spreading heavily contagious illnesses such as resistant infections that can only be treated with expensive, state-of-the-art drugs. By supplying housing to people, we are not forced to trip over a sea of people living in public parks and thoroughfares. We act as though we are helping the poor, but we are really giving only enough to deal with our own perceived problems, and thereby really benefit ourselves.

I am convinced that deep down inside we all want the poor to be cared for, we just don't want to have to pay for the care from our own individual resources by force of government or anyone else. This doesn't mean that left to our own devices we would voluntarily give over the resources necessary to end poverty either. Most people would simply expect the financially rich to do this for us anyway and thus we'd re-experience the same conditions that lead to the installation of government welfare in the first place. Leaving the care of the poor to society has been tried before and was proven insufficient to meet the needs of the majority that didn't want the poor littering the streets.

The positive results of social welfare systems would seem to be necessary in order for the middle class and wealthy to have any decent standard of living themselves. So when we complain that people should not have free access to such things, what we are really saying is that we prefer to deal with these people as did Ebenezer Scrooge and simply let them live and die off in the streets in order to reduce the surplus population. Even the staunchest adversary of taxation that I know of would not refuse to feed the poor and give them medical care if they did not have to pay for it themselves and if it did not represent a burden to anyone else. That scenario is exactly what I propose, at no cost to anyone, by simply redesigning the monetary system. Imagine, no-one would have to feel guilty any more about the poor under the systems I propose. Each person that we save represents a new consumer who spends money to stimulate our economy and must therefore be saved so that the rich still have customers to buy their goods and services and the middle class still have jobs.

Another humorous argument that I hear is that poor people, by sitting at home and not working, cause a big problem for our economy. Well, perhaps under the current taxation system they do represent a load (burden) on the working class, however, for both the rich and the middle class and the farmers, I would think that welfare and food stamp recipients would at least be acknowledged as a class of consumers that helps to keep business going and stimulate buying in the economy.

I find these arguments really funny when you consider that we are willing to go to war and expend outrageously expensive munitions, for which we receive no economic return other than the creation of jobs. During the 2007 surge of U.S. troops in the Iraq war what eventually led to the reduction of violence in the streets from 2008 through 2012 were payments of over $400,000,000 USD made by the U.S. to Sunni rebels in Iraq to maintain peace. We are willing spend this money to create peace elsewhere, but at the same time spending on welfare for the poor in our own country is somehow seen as being of little value to our stability or to our economy. These arguments simply don't hold water and they are the result of frustration for having to pay high taxes, which is seen by many as having their pockets picked (which I do understand).

What some people are only now beginning to see is the relationship between the amount of money that we commit to overcoming poverty both in developed countries and elsewhere and how that improves National Security. People who are well fed, educated and cared for are less likely to revolt against their governments, or wage war against another country.

The problem is not welfare and social security, the problem is the system itself and there is a simple cure for this problem that can be achieved by using one or more of any of the solutions outlined in this book. One must simply recognize that the true value of money is derived by thoughts, decisions and volition, and not by any other tangibles or intangibles as many have been led to believe.

Chapter 23: Education vs. Prison

Education for as many people as possible is key to a society that offers a healthy and peaceful co-existence. The founding fathers of the U.S. believed that the education of citizens was necessary for the republic to function without excessive force of government. In 1776 John Adams wrote, "Laws for the liberal education of youth, especially of the lower class of people, are so extremely wise and useful, that, to a human and generous mind, no expense for this purpose would be thought extravagant."

In the United States we have a crisis in education, particularly higher education. The driving force behind the crisis is, as usual, money. The cost of attending college today in the U.S. is so exorbitant that most people are prohibited from attending.

I am not a fan of the idea of government running schools of any kind and some believe that government financing of schools is akin to letting the fox guard the hen house. On the other hand if I had to choose between having state funded colleges and universities, where anyone could afford to attend, or, to have the system that is in place in the United States today, where commercial focus and financial necessity has transformed the college and university experience into a veritable "for profit" party vacation destination, which one can hardly even afford to attend, then I would choose to have well funded state financed colleges and universities.

It is bad enough that our antiquated economies do not guarantee that jobs will even be available for college graduates but that the cost of attending higher education is keeping people out of university and "dumbing down" our society to the extent that, for many, crime and prison have taken the place of higher education to become the new college. If there is no other reason for adequately funded state universities to exist consider that if they were still sufficiently funded today as they were in the past then higher education would be more affordable and accessible. The existence of well funded state universities would act as a deterrent for the unrestrained escalation of the costs and commercialization of private education that we are experiencing today.

Since the administration of Abraham Lincoln the U.S. funded state colleges and the practice of funding education further continued as every administration in the U.S. saw the value in having educated citizens. From 1956 through 1975 the state of California was the nation's leader in education, sparing no expense on a very sophisticated network of primary schools, community colleges and universities that guaranteed everyone could afford to go all the way through to obtain a high quality university education.

The beginning of the decline in higher public education in the U.S. started when the celebrated politician Ronald Reagan became governor of the state of California. He identified the costs of education to be an area where government could save money and began cutting back. Amazingly Regan ran for president with defunding U.S. colleges as part of his public political platform and went to work on the project at the federal level as soon as he was elected President. By playing to the distrust many taxpayers have of government controlled education, the politicians of the day convinced voters to go along with the defunding of public education and leave it to banks and commercial interests to provide funding.

It's not enough that bankers make a profit on virtually all real estate transactions in the U.S., because few can afford to buy property without a loan, but they have tapped into every aspect of the American Dream, including education. Banks saw the opportunity with government guaranteed student loan programs to turn a profit from the work of students and joined the lobby to defund education. Whether students could get jobs to pay for student loans or not, the U.S. government agreed it would pay back the money loaned to students with interest. At that point, the game was on to get as much profit from the taxpayers and students as could be had, and the product of education sold itself.

The irony of this policy is that not only is the U.S. government now stuck with paying back hundreds of billions of dollars worth of student loans to banks, which students can't afford to pay back, but the outcome of this debacle is that the now indirect cost of higher education to the U.S. government has skyrocketed. The difference is that now the government is paying additional fees and interest to banks (new middlemen) for the service of funding higher education AND the government is paying 5 or 6 times more in tuition from indirect funding than when the federal government simply handed out subsidies to state universities so that people could attend for free.

Another sad reality is that as the funding for higher education was being reduced by the U.S. government under the reign of President Regan another competing expense was introduced and spearheaded by Senator Ted Kennedy. It was supported by all political parties under the slogan of being "tough on crime" (and who could argue about being tough on crime). This competing expense was the introduction of the draconian U.S. Criminal Sentencing Guidelines, which was also mimicked by most states level governments. It virtually ensures that almost every American will have an equal opportunity to spend time prison, whether deserving or not, whether guilty or innocent. Since the introduction of these laws the U.S. prison population has also skyrocketed and the U.S. now has more prisoners than any other country in the world and has the highest incarceration rate in the world per capita. The business of prisons is flourishing in the U.S.

The U.S. has effectively defunded education in favor of building and maintaining more prisons. Even in prison virtually all credible opportunities for people to be rehabilitated, develop a trade or obtain any kind of education at all has been eliminated and U.S. prisons have turned into debilitating storage spaces for human beings, where retribution is more important than restitution. There a competition at work to see what business can sell more products to prisoners and store prisoners at a lower cost, with less security, less food, less space, less clothing, less visits, less T.V., less donations and less of anything that may be used to develop the mind, body or spirit.

Obviously the monetary systems that I present in this book would provide for everyone to go to public or private schools and would allow as much government spending on education as would be needed to build the best education systems in the world (no, current U.S. education is no longer the best). In addition, adopting these monetary systems would provide the money to work on effective crime prevention as well as alternatives to incarceration. Prisons could be turned back into places where real rehabilitation and education of prisoners gives them a chance to be productive members of society, rather than more dysfunctional and debilitated from time spent incarcerated.

How long are we going to make excuses for not implementing the systems in this book? How many more generations do we have to imprison and debilitate before we wake up and change the course of our economic practices? We are going to have to move to new solutions someday, so why not today?

Chapter 24: Conclusion

We have unintentionally made ourselves slaves to money rather than exploiting the tool of money to help improve the existence of everyone in the world. Money is a tool invented by us to be molded and used by us for our own convenience. Economics is also the study of human behavior, and because behavior changes, so do the rules of the science of economics. We can and should design our economic systems to suit our needs as required at any point in time.

We are finally at an age where technology and communications can facilitate the elimination of poverty and individual taxation. We can allow for the accumulation of financial wealth and provision for those who cannot accumulate or choose not to focus their lives on the accumulation of financial wealth. The same governmental systems that protect property rights can also compensate people who are disadvantaged by the system of property ownership that is automatically imposed on everyone from the time of their birth.

In this book I have provided a framework that can help usher in an improved lifestyle for the poor while taking nothing from the rich. I've presented monetary systems and practical tools that will improve the utility of government and use of business for everyone in such a way as to not place a burden on anyone.

The only things that are keeping us from moving ahead with these solutions are flawed thinking based on antiquated slogans and false beliefs that have been imbedded into our thoughts. In order for us to realize our true individual potential as human beings and as a race all we need to do is to step outside of our old ways of thinking and make a new choice for tomorrow. It may not be easy, it may be very hard work, but the time has come to do this work or risk the health and welfare and the very existence of the entire human race on Earth.

My wish is for the human race to move ahead and not backwards. It is time for us all realize our true potential and to concern ourselves with things that are more important than just making ends meet financially.

Chapter 25: Questions And Answers (Q&A)

1. Under this monetary system what would be the role of the U.S. Federal Reserve? The U.S. Federal Reserve would perform the same services that it already performs today except that instead of the U.S. Treasury borrowing money from the U.S. Federal Reserve, the U.S. Treasury would simply direct the Fed to issue money as needed to each citizen and to the U.S. Treasury. Profits made by the Fed through interest on lending and from any other sources would still be paid to the U.S. Treasury as it is today. In order to reduce the money supply directly, the U.S. Treasury may from time to time direct the Fed to dispose of money earned. The Fed would also still be in charge of adjusting interest rates as may be necessary. For example, the 100 year analysis provided in Appendix A requires that insurance companies earn at least 8% of their money under management in order to pay out all of the life insurance policies that are taken out by the U.S. Government. If this ever needs to be adjusted, or if it proves too burdensome, then the Fed could raise lending rates in order to help ensure that the insurance companies can meet their return on investment targets. On the other hand the government could elect to not receive any interest back on its expenditures on each citizen and thereby eliminate the need for such interest rate changes altogether.

2. What would happen to the Social Security Administration under this new system? The Social Security Administration would be responsible for administering payments and making determinations as to individual citizens' additional benefit amounts based on their medical or other special needs.

3. What would happen to the IRS? The IRS could continue to exist in order to collect property taxes, import/export taxes and estate taxes and/or to oversee payments being made to the individual states to cover the taxes being retained by the Federal Government on behalf of each of the residents of each state. There would be no reason to completely dismantle the IRS, and with its downsizing many of its employees could be absorbed into the Social Security Administration.

4. If you just pay people for doing nothing then how do you expect people to be

motivated to work or create? Many of the most valuable inventions and philosophies that we can identify today were developed by people who had time available. The closer the most relevant inventions occur to our present date the more easy it is to associate a monetary value of the time spent on creating a new invention, philosophy or business. This is the very reason why the first step in many great businesses and inventions today typically involves some kind of capital raising efforts. It is not possible for anyone to spend time creating or inventing unless they have the money to survive during this process. As a former investment banker I learned from experience that there is nothing that will derail the development of a new invention faster than forcing the inventors to spend their time trying to raise money to pay for their own subsistence. Human resources are usually the largest expense in any new business venture. The idea that money or financial wealth is the single greatest motivating force behind invention is erroneous. Even if it were true, money would still have to come from somewhere in order to pay someone for their time during development. Behind virtually every well known business today you will find that the founders had the ability to devote a great deal of their time towards the creation of their product and in each case the money came from some source, perhaps an existing business, an investor, a wealthy relative, a trust fund, from the estate passed down from a deceased relative, payments from unemployment insurance and even from food stamps. By enabling people to spend time on doing what they love we are creating the possibility for countless new inventions that would never had gotten off the ground because a person was working long hours at some mundane job. Will everyone want to work? No. But that does not mean that they make no positive contributions to society. As discussed throughout this book they have value to the economy as consumers. Doing good work is noble virtue that helps us to maintain health and happiness. The concept should be promoted in our society.

5. How do new monetary systems in this book relate to a resource base economy? I think that the idea of a resource based economy makes sense. I think that the implementation of my system is the first stepping stone that will force into existence a resource conscious economy. Perhaps not exactly in the way envisioned by the creators of the concept of a resource based economy, but an implementation that closely resembles it. I am unaware of any practical roadmap that would facilitate a resource based economy given the present differences in the interests of the various countries of the world. However, I can think of no better way to usher in an intensive effort to utilize the resources of the globe more efficiently than to force the suppliers to respond in the most economically advantageous way to an abrupt demand for their raw materials that will suddenly arise when millions of people all over the world are given money to spend and provided with the means to improve their standards of living. The strain on the world economy and the world resources that will result from a new source of consumers will force new thinking on the distribution of global resources and fuel new businesses that help to clean, maintain and protect the environment in a way that enables business instead of interfering with pursuits of business. The good news is that the money will also be available to help keep the environment clean and increase effectiveness of the global resource supply chain.

6. Price controls are not part of a truly capitalist system and they have been proven to fail in the past. So are you an enemy of the free market? It is unclear whether any temporary or permanent price controls will be necessary at all. I do not call for permanent price controls; I simply suggest that price controls are another tool that can be used to ease the transition to the new system as required. I believe that fixing currency rates of exchange will ultimately be the best solution and that this practice is essential. As a more extreme measure, fixing the price of one or more commodities such as gold may have the same helpful effect as restoring the gold standard; however, it is my hope that taking such a measure would also be unnecessary. I believe that eventually this would not be desirable either. The world is not a perfect place and neither is the implementation of any economic philosophy. The practice of the purest form of capitalism depends upon the opinions of those who practice it. If the U.S. represents the best implementation of capitalism, then we must accept the reality that the U.S. continues to employ a wide range of price controls. Some price controls that have been implemented in the past were obvious and include events such as the rationing of food and price controls established on foods during times of war. Other price controls include restrictions on the price of oil and even the declaration of the amount of gold that one dollar used to represent when the U.S. dollar was based on a gold standard. Some price controls have helped to achieve desired results while many have not. There are many price controls still in use today and price controls appear to be an unavoidable part of virtually every economic system that has existed. Today price controls still continue in the U.S. in both direct and indirect forms including, tax breaks that encourage people to invest in real estate and oil and help fuel the property and resource bubbles. Directives of the Federal Trade Commission continually involve direct regulation of prices of services and products through enforcement actions. Securities and Exchange Commission trading halts of suspect securities and intraday trading lock limits imposed on commodities by the Commodity Futures Trading Commission. During the last 2008 recession there were days when short selling was not allowed in the stock market. The list goes on and on. Rather than debating semantics of the concepts I believe that it is more important to come up with solutions to our existing faulty economic and monetary systems where price controls are already in use every day. Furthermore the implementation of the solutions to our economic woes must be designed to harm or offend as few people as possible (if anyone at all). I believe that the solutions that I propose harm no-one and empower everyone. The implementation of the monetary policies in this book may require the temporary or even permanent fixing, by law, of prices of various commodities within the U.S. such as gold, fuel or food products. Then again no formal price limits may need to be imposed depending on the reaction of the economy to so many new people suddenly being empowered with more money to spend.

7. This will never work. Do you honestly believe that the bankers, the rich and politicians who control the world would pay people for nothing? I believe that it is in the best interests of bankers, the rich and politicians to give people money to buy and use the products and services that they or their social classes sell. I can see no downside for any of these groups that would occur by the implementation of my system. I can see a great relief from the burden of being forced to pay some existing taxes. I see an opportunity for the resurgence of respect and admiration for the government and even patriotism and even support of business rather than condemnation as byproducts of the implementation of my systems. I believe the majority of the people in the world would be extraordinarily happy of the new system.

8. Do you expect the government and the intelligence community to willingly give up the information that they collect about people and the control over people's lives that comes from their tax returns? The advent of new technology enables the collection of this data in new ways. In order to retain access to this information the government could require recipients of the monthly stipend to supply them with annual reports of virtually any kind in order to receive the benefits. My hope is that no such reporting would be necessary, but I imagine that many people would produce such reports and agree to do other things if necessary in order to receive a stipend. Again, given modern technology and new surveillance techniques I don't see any of this as necessary any more. I'm sure that new creative ways will be found by the intelligence community to continue to collect the information that they already collect.

9. If you give people money then won't they just tear apart the houses that they rent like they do in the government low income

housing programs? Not everyone will tear up houses that they rent. It cannot be proven that everyone who receives money from my program will revert to a lower animal level of consciousness. In my system we could do away with government subsidized housing programs because people would have enough money to pay rent. I believe the problems associated with programs such as government subsidized housing are the rules imposed by such programs. I also believe that the behavior of people depends largely on how they are raised by their parents which is a topic beyond the scope of this book.

10. If everyone is given $1,620 USD per month who would be left to work at fast food restaurants? $1,620 USD per month does not provide a high standard of living, just a basic existence. There will still be people who are qualified to work at fast food restaurants and people who want to eat fast food. The only difference would be that under my proposed stipend system people could work at lower paying jobs and have high enough standards of living that would enable them to work in such jobs by choice and with dignity rather than working at those kinds of jobs out of necessity. A happy work force that is not worried about how they will make ends meet will likely provide a higher quality of service when they work at a job by choice rather than because of necessity.

11. What would happen to the minimum wage? I believe that we should keep the minimum wage. There will need to be a minimum wage to protect non-citizens who work in our country and do not receive a government stipend. I also believe that the minimum wage could be reduced by 1/3 when paying people who receive the government stipend. This would inspire business managers to hire workers that are citizens of our own country rather than sending jobs overseas. Hiring people who do not receive a government stipend would also require that the employer pay for their medical care. By implementing the systems I propose it reduces the need for us to police our boarders for any reason other than defense purposes. By using the systems I propose there would be no reason to prevent those with no criminal background from coming to our country because they would have a harder time getting work here because it would be more expensive for employers to hire them. Having foreigners in our country would not interfere with any of our social programs or financial standards of living and thus an entire class of problems associated with immigration would be solved. Citizenship or permanent residency would be the only paths for people to gain access to the government stipend.

12. Why should people get something for nothing? I agree, people should not get something for nothing. This is why those who enjoy the exclusive use of the property that they perceive that they own need to compensate those people who were automatically denied use of the same property because of the system of government that existed since their birth. The prevailing purpose of government around the world is to protect and segregate rights to use of property. In other words, under the systems that I propose people are not being paid for nothing, they are being paid a small stipend that enables them to rent (or buy) the very same property which was automatically taken away from them at birth and is being protected by force of law and government authority. Because people are no longer free to simply live off the land, because the land is owned by individuals, corporations and ultimately the governments, there needs to be some provision that compensates people in some way that makes up for their automatic loss of the right to utilize public and privately held land in order to grow food and build shelter to survive. So people are not being given something for nothing, but under our current system something has already been taken away from each person whose parents did not own land and/or property that was passed down to them. In our current system the only people who are presently those who have received something for nothing are those people who have been born into wealth or inherited it. The lack of compensation for the taking away of property from some people is a fundamental flaw in our current system of government that negatively affects the rich and poor. I am not proposing that we take from the rich and give to the poor, or that every person should be made to have equal wealth or property, I am simply saying that the current system is so out of balance that those who posses wealth indirectly impose a lifestyle of servitude on those who are not born into wealth and this results in economic and lifestyle instability for everyone. It is a problem that is simple to cure by simply building into the existing system some facility to compensate people in such a way so that they can rent or purchase what they would otherwise have access to (rent and food) directly from the land if the government did not exist. Who should pay this compensation? The government that is the very mechanism that creates the problem in the first place. The rich need not pay because the government has the facility to create money that has value by force of law and so the government can pay. In other words, the problems that result by the institution of government can also be fixed by the government if we all agree to simply continue to use U.S. dollars that are backed by full faith in the U.S. Government, which is what we already practice.

13. How do you expect private life insurance companies to pay the government back the same money that they paid to people and what about some people who are so unhealthy that they are uninsurable? I propose the benefit payable to the government from these insurance annuities only be equal to the amounts that were paid out by the government to each individual being insured, and may perhaps include a modest profit. I discourage the idea of the profit because it could eventually compound the amounts of profit needed to be made by insurance companies to unsustainable levels. People would have the option to refuse their monthly stipend or to have it paid to someone else. For people who are uninsurable, we would increase the premiums paid for people who are insurable in order to make up the difference. This model has been used successfully by commercial businesses that purchase life insurance for their employees and profit from the practice today.

14. Implementation of this new system could cause prices of certain commodities, products and services to skyrocket, what then? Our current economic systems already cause prices of commodities to fluctuate through irrational and damaging levels. If, under the new system costs of food and other critical infrastructure increases to levels that threaten the very same things that we are trying to provide access to then the government will need to do what it has done many times in the past which is institute temporary or permanent price controls until the systems stabilize.

15. Your currency boundary association sounds like you are creating the evil one world government that is prophesied as playing a role in the destruction of the world? We have successfully relied on currency rate control agreements in past such as the Bretton Woods Accord that did not lead to a one world government scenario and thus I do not believe that this will result from doing a similar thing again. While such associations can be used to sanction nations in a similar manner to the way the United Nations already imposes sanctions on nations, the governments of nations will always be sovereign and will always be able to withdraw from any such association. The stronger the nation is the easier it would be to withdraw from the proposed currency association and therefore all countries will ultimately retain their own autonomy. The purpose of participating in the association is to gain a benefit of currency stability and if that benefit is outweighed by any requirements imposed on the member nations. Members will be free to withdraw at any time and allow their currency to "float" in value again. It is also possible that various nations may unite into various currency rate control agreements outside of the currency rate control association founded by G7 and NATO member nations. The idea of a one world government would require each individual country to surrender complete control of its government to one authority. This is not what I am proposing in this book.

16. Why don't we just go back to the gold standard? History has demonstrated that implementations of currencies that are redeemable for a commodity are impractical. There are several reasons. One of these reasons is the arbitrary nature of the occurrence of the commodities themselves. For example if one country has more gold deposits than another then that country is automatically placed at an advantage for no reason other than luck. Another reason is because of the high costs associated with storing, transporting and the redemption processes of such commodities. And perhaps one of the most important reasons why commodity based currencies have been abandoned is because ultimately the supply of commodity itself is not sufficient when compared to the growth of the population of the world and can therefore not sufficiently capitalize everyone that is alive. Using a gold based currency requires the price controls by virtue of the fact that laws are passed that state that one dollar is redeemable for a specific amount of gold. The problem with past implementations of the gold standard is the redeemable aspect that requires the government (or banks) to surrender gold to the holder of a dollar bill on demand. Since I am not opposed to the use of price controls, I do see one possible way to successfully return the U.S. dollar to a rate that is tied to gold. I am not completely opposed to the idea of returning to a currency whose price is set by the price of gold only because it would be an improvement over what exists today. But I see no point in doing so because there are much more efficient ways to manage the real problem and because there may come a time when mining for gold becomes more expensive than whatever valuation is used to fix a unit of currency to an ounce of gold. Nonetheless, the new improved method of returning to a gold standard would require a simple act of law that would state that no buying or selling of gold or import or export of gold could take place within the U.S. above a certain U.S. dollar amount per ounce. In this way the U.S. Government could permanently attach the value of the U.S. dollar to some amount of gold if it wanted to without ever having to worry about how much money was in circulation or without having to worry about storing gold or the process of redeeming money for gold. Again, I don't see any benefit to this measure unless the high price of gold caused some eminent threat to economic stability. What I believe is much more important is to establish the rate of exchange of currencies between countries rather than arbitrarily fix currency rates on some commodity.

17. I think that using life insurance on people is immoral. Don't you think that your plan that is based so heavily on life insurance will inspire people to kill for profit? Of course any system can be abused. Of course some business owners may try to kill people if businesses use insurance policies on their employees, but I think the overall majority of those who would benefit from the system would far outweigh practices that are already against the law and immoral. We do not abandon the practice of using cars even though thousands of people are killed in them every year and even though they are sometimes used as weapons by insane people. There will always be murderers but this is an issue that has more to do with education, environment and law enforcement than whether or not people use life insurance as a positive tool.

18. There are some people that believe that

using any of these methods, particularly the Dot method, will lead to a one world government and a one world currency that is predicted in religious prophecies to precede the coming of the anti-Christ and the end of the world. What do you think? I don't believe this is the case at all and here are the reasons why:

a. In the first place worrying about this is of no use because if you believe that these prophecies are destined to come true then it will not matter whether or not we create any new currencies or change how our current monetary system works because there will be nothing that we will be able to do to prevent the prophecies from coming true anyway. Whether a change in monetary policy happens before or after such end times would be irrelevant if the end times are going to happen anyway. No one could say for certain if the implementation of any of these monetary systems would hasten the fulfillment of the prophecies or actually delay them. No-one who believes the prophesies could know for sure how any of these things would happen; they could only be assured that they would come to pass. Even Christ stated that only the Father knows when these things will happen not us.

b. I am not requiring that we completely do away with the fluctuation of currency exchange rates, but rather I propose that we establish and maintain upper and lower boundaries for these rates in order to provide for a higher degree of global economic stability. Similar policies have already been successfully used in the past with the Bretton Woods Accord and we did not usher in the end of the world.

c. I am not proposing a one world centralized government or the elimination of any of the existing currencies. The sanctions that can be facilitated by currency exchange rate associations would simply provide for more effective sanctions than are already used by the United Nations. The United Nations would be more likely to be used as a means of centralized global government than the institution of one or more currency exchange rate associations.

d. Any country would be able to resign from any currency exchange rate association that they belonged to at any time and thus each member country would retain their independence at all times.

e. Individuals or groups of people who are banned from receiving the monthly stipend or from using Dots or who elected not to participates in either would be free to use any of the currencies of their home country and the rest of the world and thus they would still be able to buy and sell.

f. I am not proposing that people be stamped with any numbers, bar codes or other symbols as in the numbers of "The Beast."

g. I believe that if such predictions of one world government being ruled by an anti-Christ do come to pass then it will require a formal and thorough voluntary relinquishment or a taking by force the control both of nations and individuals regardless of the nature of their monetary policies.

h. The current construct of our economic systems lend themselves far more easily to abuse and usurpation of power then what I propose.

19. Throughout your book you cite the Bretten Woods Accords. The Bretton Woods system is usually cited as evidence of the fragility of fixed exchange-rate systems, so why do you reference it as an example of good practice? I proposed a modified version of currency rate controls that involves constant analysis and agreements between participants in the association that is fluid rather than constant. Thus my proposal cures the problems that arose in the Bretton Woods version of the currency rate controls, while providing the benefits that lead me to site the old Accord. Instead of me answering your question by myself, let me refer you to the answers provided by the Minneapolis branch of the U.S. Federal Reserve in an essay from the synopsis of the Minneapolis Fed's 1989 Annual Report, authored by Warren E. Weber, manager of the Research Department's monetary studies section, and Arthur J. Rolnick, director of research who said,

"...Bretton Woods is not really a test of whether a fixed exchange-rate system will work. A fixed-rate system requires that policy coordination include an agreement among countries about the amount of seigniorage and its distribution. This component of policy coordination was missing from the Bretton Woods system, which attempted to fix exchange rates while allowing each country some control of its own seigniorage. A proper test of whether fixed exchange rates are feasible needs evidence from a system with the two required components of policy coordination in place. Such a system exists, and it is running smoothly—the monetary system of the United States."

Obviously I disagree with the part above about the monetary system of the U.S. running smoothly. I contend it is anything but smooth, but it does prove how value can be managed as stated in the quote above.

20. The government tried paying everyone in the communist system in Russia and look at that disaster. Are you a communist? The monetary system that I introduce in this book is independent of the labels of communist or capitalist and can thus be utilized by a government that uses almost any political structure including statist, capitalism, socialism, communism or oligarchy like the U.S.. To try to compare my monetary system to capitalism or communism is like trying to insert a chapter on birds into a book on geography. In order to further illustrate how the systems that I propose would not change the capitalist economy of the U.S. I have created a chart below that compares the components of my system to The Former Soviet Union, Present Day Cuba, Present Day China and the United States.

COMPARISON OF THE NEW PROPOSED MONETARY SYSTEMS TO OLD AND PRESENT DAY PRACTICES OF GOVERNMENTS					
# GOVERNMENT PROVIDES, ALLOWS or ENGAGES IN	U.S.S.R.	CUBA	CHINA	U.S.A.	New Sys. In U.S.A.
1 VOTE FOR LEADERS	Limited	Limited	Limited	Yes	Yes
2 INCOME TAX	No	Yes as of 2013	Yes	Yes	No
3 VALUE ADDED TAX	Yes as of 1992	Yes	Yes	No	Optional
4 FOOD ASSISTANCE	Yes	Yes	No	Yes	Yes
5 MEDICAL CARE ASSISTANCE	Yes	Yes	Yes	Yes	Yes
6 HOUSING ASSISTANCE	Yes	Yes	Yes	Yes	Yes
7 CASH ASSISTANCE	Yes	Yes	Yes	Yes	Yes
8 EDUCATION ASSISTANCE	Yes	Yes	Yes	Yes	Yes
9 REDISTROBUTION OF WEALTH	Yes	Yes	Yes	Yes	No
10 RELIGEOUS FREEDOM	No	Limited	Limited	Yes	Yes
11 FREEDOM TO TRAVEL	No	Yes as of 2012	Yes as of 2005	Yes	Yes

21. People are lazy; they cannot have things handed to them and so the system is immoral. Aren't you afraid of contributing to the decay of the masses? Rich people and their children don't need to work and there are many of them who have made vital contributions to society throughout history and have led exemplary lives. Reality T.V. and social media is fond of providing entertainment by broadcasting the seemingly wasted lives and bad behavior of "trust fund" children and other wealthy teenagers and young adults. In addition, social media also makes a spectacle of the lives of some people who live dependant on welfare payments and grow up living in the decay of government subsidized housing without sufficient education and without decent parenting. The good deeds and exemplary lives of the majority of law abiding and responsible people from both of these groups do not appear to be entertaining enough to broadcast on television. As a result we see only shows where people are irresponsible and we are thus left with the false idea that all people who are wealthy or poor fall into these stereotypes. While these reality shows and media stories make intoxicating entertainment for many people they have little to do with how people survive financially and have everything to do with the subject of parenting and values. The subjects of parenting and values are beyond the scope of this book except that I would say that, based on my experience, good parents tend to educate themselves continually about their jobs as parents and thus they raise children that grow into responsible adults regardless of whether or not they grow up on welfare or on a trust fund or have to work to make a living. I'll leave you with the following examples of a few wealthy famous people that come to mind who lived exemplary lives. Augusta Ada King, Countess of Lovelace who was an English mathematician who lived in the early 19th century and who is credited as the world's first computer programmer led a dignified and exemplary life. She was able to do this in spite of the fact that she was the daughter of the famous poet Lord Byron who was celebrated for aristocratic excesses, including huge debts, numerous love affairs with both sexes, rumors of a scandalous liaison with his half-sister, and self-imposed exile. Another example is Charles Babbage who was a mathematician, philosopher, inventor and mechanical engineer, who is best remembered now for originating the concept of a programmable computer. I could go on and on by providing examples of wealthy people who did not have to work and who made great contributions throughout history however it would take up too much space. For those who believe that receiving welfare will lead to lethargy I've provided short list of some contemporary and successful people who had once benefited from food stamps: Jan Koum who sold his company, WhatsApp, to Facebook for $19 billion; Bruce Springsteen, Sen. Patty Murray, the four-term Democrat from Washington; The mother of Dr. Ben Carson the famous doctor and conservative; Celebrity Chef Sandra Lee; President Barack Obama's mother Ann Dunham; The mother of Mike McCue, the founder and CEO of the app Flipboard; Craig T. Nelson the actor and former "Coach" star; Rep. Barbara Lee, the California Democrat ; Moby, the musical artist ; Phil Drake, the president of Drake Enterprises, Ltd. and a fervent conservative and a tea party enthusiast; Kyle Abraham, the choreographer and recent recipient of a MacArthur Foundation "genius grant". Many people are quick to reference the resourcefulness of people like millionaire Chris Gardner, who inspired the movie "The Pursuit of Happiness," who was homeless with a young son while he was in a finance training program as a model for what all people who are poor should strive to be. However, despite enjoying the movie myself, I don't believe that the actions taken by the star would be easily duplicated or even attempted by many people under similar circumstances. It should also be noted that the success of many celebrated business people and investors such as Donald Trump and Bill Gates would not have been possible without the financial backing of their parents. My point in saying this is that many success stories were simply the result of having the right resources at the right time and that charity and government aid programs can provide the resources that are necessary for some people to make that leap from poverty to success in the very same way that investors pay the salary

211

of upstart companies.

22. Doesn't the Bible encourage people to work hard, take care of themselves and to avoid taking hand outs? Why should anything be given to anyone? There is no question that performing good work is a noble ethic that is proven to be healthy for people that should always be promoted. The Bible says that you can tell all about people by the fruits they bare (what they produce). However, in the first place, because of the way our systems of modern government are designed something has already been taken away from people who are not born into families that have property and access to wealth. What has been taken away is their basic right to live on land (property), cultivate the land and use it to survive at no monetary cost to them. The system proposed is not designed to make people rich or to discourage them from doing any work but simply compensates people with a minimum amount necessary for the use of their share of property by others by providing them with some means to have access to (rent/own) something that they would have otherwise had access to which is a place to sleep, food and the ability to travel from one place to another without human obstruction. This compensation is simply taking place in a way that is commensurate with modern day technologies, capabilities and standards of living. In regards to the Bible, few people can claim that they can truly live up to the spirit of the scriptures of Bible such as, Matthew 19:21 where Jesus said, "If you want to be perfect, go, sell your possessions and give to the poor, and you will have treasure in heaven. Then come, follow me." While the Bible does speak of work, it does not specify how hard the work has to be or the specific amount of hard work that must be done in order to survive. The Bible does not command us to take jobs that we don't like but rather to do good work in whatever jobs we do. There is a difference between work and slavery as in Exodus 5:4-18. There is the famous scripture of 2 Thessalonians 3:6-12 which ends with this charge, "If anyone is not willing to work, let him not eat," however, this scripture is given in the context of not being a burden to others, "For you yourselves know how you ought to imitate us, because we were not idle when we were with you, nor did we eat anyone's bread without paying for it, but with toil and labor we worked night and day, that we might not be a burden to any of you. " Unlike the most popular and current welfare systems in the world that tax the rich to pay for the poor, the monetary system that I propose does not place any burden on anyone and is not discouraging anyone from working, but rather facilitating the possibility of working on what you truly love or taking a job not out of necessity but out of choice. Rather than me preach to anyone, I leave it to you to decide for yourself what the Bible is saying about welfare and my proposed system, which is unlike our current welfare system in that it takes from no-one but provides a minimum standard of living. In appendix C I have provided some scriptures from the Bible that appear to be applicable to welfare for your own analysis and interpretation.

23. Instead of implementing your plans in this book, couldn't the U.S. Government just pay the national debt with a newly minted currency or note in one swoop or just pass a law to turn the national debt back to zero? Yes, the U.S. Government could do this and it would only serve to prove that the solutions that I provide in this book are viable, but cancelling the national debt in this way would not solve the problems that got us into the situation in the first place. In my opinion it would be a cop-out if they did not implement the payments to people and cancel the tax system because it would be like saying, "yes we acknowledge that we have the power to create money from nothing and wipe out debt," and at the same time saying, "But we are not going to pay people for doing nothing and we are not going to create money for your benefit." If this were to take place then in my opinion it would be a sign that there really is some kind of conspiracy or other force at work that will not allow people to live in anything other than servitude.

24. It's not good for people to become dependent on government. Won't people be at risk if they rely on the government for their day to day survival? Dependency on the government for our day to day survival is already an inescapable part of the life of every person today, rich or poor. We are all reliant on our government to provide for the protection of our property and lives. We are reliant on the government to provide roads, law enforcement, the military, schooling, unemployment insurance payments, welfare programs, social security, medical care for the elderly, regulation of various businesses, and protection of our borders. The list of things that we all depend on from government goes on and on. The only question is whether or not you would like to continue paying taxes for these things and continue to stand by and watch the current system fail until everyone is in need of government assistance. Or the alternative is to adopt a monetary system that automatically increases the quality of life for everyone at no cost to anyone and restores the actual utility of government. There is no reason to live in denial when it comes to everyone's dependency on government nor is it good for the government to regulate the use and access to property without compensating those who are displaced by it. This is not a system designed to give something away for free, but to restore something that has already been taken away from everyone, which is the default right to use property and to "live off the land."

25. Your Dot system appears to take control of the creation of money and provide it to the users of money rather than the elite bankers that control the oligarchy of governments today. Do you seriously expect them to go along with this? I do not pretend to know or understand if these conspiratorial people, groups or forces exist in any cooperative form. I often think that the sheer stupidity and crazy real life characters that often prevail in the theater of public policies does seem to support the notion of an evil collective that puppet masters the world. My experience in the financial world and in working with certain government agencies has provided me with a first-hand knowledge of some of the forces that do actually govern the world and our economics systems and in fact we are already headed in the direction of economics based on the principles revealed in this book. As a Consciousness Coach I have come to the opinion that the collective selfishness of each individual tends to be the source of the real evils that manifest in the world. However where such controlling entities do seriously exist I do expect them to allow for the Dot system for several reasons. The first reason is that they will still control the creation of the individual currencies of their own countries. Secondly, the introduction of the monetary policies that I propose do not displace any of the current already existing concentrations of financial wealth they simply improve the entire market space and the quality of life for everyone, including the supposed clandestine rulers of the world (i.e. The Illuminate, etc.). I have no doubt in my mind that if there is a "collective" conspiratorial force or group that controls the destiny of the money system and world governments (other than the actual ignorance of mankind itself) that this same force or group of controllers will find a new way to retain their dominance over society using these new systems and will even have their usual fun in the process of implementing the new systems.

For every disease that is cured another takes its place, for every enemy that is defeated another arises to take its place. For whatever reason it appears that dealing with adversity is part of the human experience of life and I do not expect those components of our existence to change just because we end might end poverty or change our money policy.

25. Where can I participate in Dot Money or find out who is working on other solutions?
For more information about Dot Money or any other of the solutions that I present in this book and keep track of go to: www.DotMoneyBook.com

APPENDIX A

An example of what the money supply would look like if life insurance was used to reduce the money supply over the next 100 years.

An example of what the money supply would look like if life insurance was used to reduce the money supply over the next 100 years.

AMOUNT PAID OUT TO EACH PERSON EACH YEAR:	$44,400
Paid to life insurance each year:	$4,800
Expected Interest Rate Paid Back (could be inflation Rate):	2.00%
Required Interest Earned by Insurance to sustain:	8.20%
Deal	0.80%
Average Life Span (Years):	80

YR	POPULATION	PAID OUT (this Year)	DEATHS	PAID BACK TO GOV	CASH IN FLOAT	PAID TO INS.	HOLDINGS BY INSURANCE CO's	AVAL./ PERSON
1	317,000,000	$14,074,800,000,000	2,540,064	$115,034,423,077	$13,959,765,576,923	$1,521,600,000,000	$1,531,336,776,923	$44,037
2	318,207,568	$14,128,416,000,000	2,549,740	$230,945,261,538	$27,857,236,315,385	$1,527,396,324,324	$3,078,603,954,011	$87,544
3	319,415,135	$14,182,032,000,000	2,559,416	$347,732,515,385	$41,691,535,800,000	$1,533,192,648,649	$4,642,231,408,693	$130,525
4	320,622,703	$14,235,648,000,000	2,569,092	$465,396,184,615	$55,461,787,615,385	$1,538,988,972,973	$6,222,684,268,348	$172,981
5	321,830,270	$14,289,264,000,000	2,578,768	$583,936,269,231	$69,167,115,346,154	$1,544,785,297,297	$7,820,465,800,797	$214,918
6	323,037,838	$14,342,880,000,000	2,588,444	$703,352,769,231	$82,806,642,576,923	$1,550,581,621,622	$9,436,120,541,826	$256,337
7	324,245,405	$14,396,496,000,000	2,598,120	$823,645,684,615	$96,379,492,892,308	$1,556,377,945,946	$11,070,237,679,154	$297,242
8	325,452,973	$14,450,112,000,000	2,607,796	$944,815,015,385	$109,884,789,876,923	$1,562,174,270,270	$12,723,454,713,893	$337,636
9	326,660,541	$14,503,728,000,000	2,617,472	$1,066,860,761,538	$123,321,657,115,385	$1,567,970,594,595	$14,396,461,422,245	$377,522
10	327,868,108	$14,557,344,000,000	2,627,148	$1,189,782,923,077	$136,689,218,192,308	$1,573,766,918,919	$16,090,004,142,062	$416,903
11	329,075,676	$14,610,960,000,000	2,636,824	$1,313,581,500,000	$149,986,596,692,308	$1,579,563,243,243	$17,804,890,410,900	$455,781
12	330,283,243	$14,664,576,000,000	2,646,500	$1,438,256,492,308	$163,212,916,200,000	$1,585,359,567,568	$19,541,993,984,395	$494,160
13	331,490,811	$14,718,192,000,000	2,656,176	$1,563,807,900,000	$176,367,300,300,000	$1,591,155,891,892	$21,302,260,266,142	$532,043
14	332,698,378	$14,771,808,000,000	2,665,852	$1,690,235,723,077	$189,448,872,576,923	$1,596,952,216,216	$23,086,712,182,835	$569,431
15	333,905,946	$14,825,424,000,000	2,675,528	$1,817,539,961,538	$202,456,756,615,385	$1,602,748,540,541	$24,896,456,541,153	$606,329
16	335,113,514	$14,879,040,000,000	2,685,204	$1,945,720,615,385	$215,390,076,000,000	$1,608,544,864,865	$26,732,690,905,927	$642,738
17	336,321,081	$14,932,656,000,000	2,694,880	$2,074,777,684,615	$228,247,954,315,385	$1,614,341,189,189	$28,596,711,042,301	$678,661
18	337,528,649	$14,986,272,000,000	2,704,556	$2,204,711,169,231	$241,029,515,146,154	$1,620,137,513,514	$30,489,918,968,160	$714,101
19	338,736,216	$15,039,888,000,000	2,714,233	$2,335,521,069,231	$253,733,882,076,923	$1,625,933,837,838	$32,413,831,666,859	$749,060
20	339,943,784	$15,093,504,000,000	2,723,909	$2,467,207,384,615	$266,360,178,692,308	$1,631,730,162,162	$34,370,090,514,385	$783,542
21	341,151,351	$15,147,120,000,000	2,733,585	$2,599,770,115,385	$278,907,528,576,923	$1,637,526,486,486	$36,360,471,479,559	$817,548
22	342,358,919	$15,200,736,000,000	2,743,261	$2,733,209,261,538	$291,375,055,315,385	$1,643,322,810,811	$38,386,896,160,641	$851,081

217

APPENDIX A (Continued)

An example of what the money supply would look like if life insurance was used to reduce the money supply over the next 100 years. (Continued)

An example of what the money supply would look like if life insurance was used to reduce the money supply over the next 100 years. (CONTINUED)

YR	POPULATION	PAID OUT (this Year)	DEATHS	PAID BACK TO GOV	CASH IN FLOAT	PAID TO INS.	HOLDINGS BY INSURANCE CO's	CASH AVAL / PERSON
23	343,565,486	$15,254,352,000,000	2,752,937	$2,867,524,823,077	$303,761,882,492,308	$1,649,119,135,135	$40,451,443,726,953	$884,143
24	344,776,054	$15,307,968,000,000	2,762,613	$3,002,716,800,000	$316,067,133,692,308	$1,654,915,459,459	$42,556,363,839,699	$916,737
25	345,988,622	$15,361,584,000,000	2,772,289	$3,138,785,192,308	$328,289,932,500,000	$1,660,711,783,784	$44,704,090,632,300	$948,865
26	347,189,189	$15,415,200,000,000	2,781,965	$3,275,730,000,000	$340,429,402,500,000	$1,666,508,108,108	$46,897,257,837,122	$980,530
27	348,394,757	$15,468,816,000,000	2,791,641	$3,413,551,223,077	$352,484,667,276,923	$1,672,304,432,432	$49,138,715,152,581	$1,011,733
28	349,606,324	$15,522,432,000,000	2,801,317	$3,552,248,861,538	$364,454,850,415,385	$1,678,100,756,757	$51,431,545,952,365	$1,042,478
29	350,811,892	$15,576,048,000,000	2,810,993	$3,691,822,915,385	$376,339,075,500,000	$1,683,897,081,081	$53,779,086,446,804	$1,072,766
30	352,015,459	$15,629,664,000,000	2,820,669	$3,832,273,384,615	$388,136,466,115,385	$1,689,693,405,405	$56,184,946,415,475	$1,102,599
31	353,222,027	$15,683,280,000,000	2,830,345	$3,973,600,269,231	$399,846,145,846,154	$1,695,489,729,730	$58,653,031,639,881	$1,131,981
32	354,434,595	$15,736,896,000,000	2,840,021	$4,115,803,569,231	$411,467,238,276,923	$1,701,286,054,054	$61,187,568,175,607	$1,160,912
33	355,642,162	$15,790,512,000,000	2,849,697	$4,258,883,284,615	$422,998,866,992,308	$1,707,082,378,378	$63,793,128,614,796	$1,189,395
34	356,849,730	$15,844,128,000,000	2,859,373	$4,402,839,415,385	$434,440,155,576,923	$1,712,878,702,703	$66,474,660,502,149	$1,217,432
35	358,057,297	$15,897,744,000,000	2,869,049	$4,547,671,961,538	$445,790,227,615,385	$1,718,675,027,027	$69,237,517,081,030	$1,245,025
36	359,264,865	$15,951,360,000,000	2,878,725	$4,693,380,923,077	$457,048,206,692,308	$1,724,471,351,351	$72,087,490,560,760	$1,272,176
37	361,680,300	$16,058,592,000,000	2,888,077	$4,856,179,984,615	$468,250,618,707,692	$1,736,064,000,000	$75,020,906,050,127	$1,294,654
38	368,446,300	$16,359,020,160,000	2,952,295	$5,080,734,145,846	$479,528,904,721,846	$1,768,542,720,000	$78,005,449,423,431	$1,301,489
39	375,212,300	$16,659,448,320,000	3,006,513	$5,310,199,152,000	$490,878,153,889,846	$1,801,021,440,000	$81,040,402,322,233	$1,308,266
40	381,979,300	$16,959,876,480,000	3,060,731	$5,544,575,003,077	$502,293,455,366,769	$1,833,500,160,000	$84,124,987,482,699	$1,314,976
41	388,745,400	$17,260,304,640,000	3,114,949	$5,783,861,699,077	$513,769,898,307,692	$1,865,978,880,000	$87,258,363,905,363	$1,321,610
42	395,512,400	$17,560,732,800,000	3,169,167	$6,028,059,240,000	$525,302,571,367,692	$1,898,457,600,000	$90,439,621,628,803	$1,328,158
43	402,278,400	$17,861,160,960,000	3,223,385	$6,277,167,625,846	$536,886,565,201,846	$1,930,936,320,000	$93,667,276,074,759	$1,334,614
44	409,044,600	$18,161,589,120,000	3,277,603	$6,531,186,856,615	$548,516,967,465,231	$1,963,415,040,000	$96,941,761,929,554	$1,340,970
45	415,811,270	$18,462,017,280,000	3,331,821	$6,790,116,932,308	$560,188,867,812,923	$1,995,893,760,000	$100,260,426,523,789	$1,347,219
46	422,577,620	$18,762,445,440,000	3,386,038	$7,053,957,852,923	$571,897,355,400,000	$2,028,372,480,000	$103,622,522,669,177	$1,353,355
47	429,344,000	$19,062,873,600,000	3,440,256	$7,322,709,618,462	$583,637,519,381,539	$2,060,851,200,000	$107,026,700,907,988	$1,359,370
48	436,110,410	$19,363,301,760,000	3,494,474	$7,596,372,228,923	$595,404,448,912,615	$2,093,329,920,000	$110,471,501,126,960	$1,365,261
49	442,876,380	$19,663,729,920,000	3,548,692	$7,874,945,684,308	$607,193,233,148,308	$2,125,808,640,000	$113,955,343,483,543	$1,371,021
50	449,643,360	$19,964,158,080,000	3,602,910	$8,158,429,984,615	$618,998,961,243,692	$2,158,287,360,000	$117,476,518,588,098	$1,376,645
51	456,409,690	$20,264,586,240,000	3,657,128	$8,446,825,129,846	$630,816,722,353,846	$2,190,766,080,000	$121,033,176,881,036	$1,382,129
52	463,176,060	$20,565,014,400,000	3,711,346	$8,740,131,120,000	$642,641,605,633,846	$2,223,244,800,000	$124,623,317,138,481	$1,387,467
53	469,942,400	$20,865,442,560,000	3,765,564	$9,038,347,955,077	$654,468,700,238,769	$2,255,723,520,000	$128,244,774,037,832	$1,392,657
54	476,708,800	$21,165,870,720,000	3,819,782	$9,341,475,635,077	$666,293,095,323,692	$2,288,202,240,000	$131,895,204,697,537	$1,397,694
55	483,475,200	$21,466,298,880,000	3,874,000	$9,649,514,160,000	$678,109,880,043,692	$2,320,680,960,000	$135,572,074,121,455	$1,402,574
56	490,241,600	$21,766,727,040,000	3,928,218	$9,962,463,529,846	$689,914,143,553,846	$2,353,159,680,000	$139,272,639,443,329	$1,407,294
57	497,008,000	$22,067,155,200,000	3,982,436	$10,280,323,744,615	$701,700,975,009,231	$2,385,638,400,000	$142,993,932,881,866	$1,411,850
58	503,774,400	$22,367,583,360,000	4,036,654	$10,603,094,804,308	$713,465,463,564,923	$2,418,117,120,000	$146,732,743,297,712	$1,416,240
59	510,540,800	$22,668,011,520,000	4,090,872	$10,930,776,708,923	$725,202,698,376,000	$2,450,595,840,000	$150,485,596,238,081	$1,420,460
60	517,307,200	$22,968,439,680,000	4,145,090	$11,263,369,458,462	$736,907,768,597,539	$2,483,074,560,000	$154,248,732,345,062	$1,424,507
61	524,073,600	$23,268,867,840,000	4,199,308	$11,600,873,052,923	$748,575,763,384,615	$2,515,553,280,000	$158,018,083,993,394	$1,428,379

APPENDIX A (Continued)

An example of what the money supply would look like if life insurance was used to reduce the money supply over the next 100 years. (Continued)

An example of what the money supply would look like if life insurance was used to reduce the money supply over the next 100 years. (CONTINUED)

YR	POPULATION	PAID OUT (this Year)	DEATHS	PAID BACK TO GOV	CASH IN FLOAT	PAID TO INS.	HOLDINGS BY INSURANCE CO's	CASH AVAL./ PERSON
62	530,840,000	$23,569,296,000,000	4,253,526	$11,943,287,492,308	$760,201,771,892,308	$2,548,032,000,000	$161,789,250,012,545	$1,432,073
63	537,606,400	$23,869,724,160,000	4,307,744	$12,290,612,776,615	$771,780,883,275,692	$2,580,510,720,000	$165,557,464,335,598	$1,435,587
64	544,372,800	$24,170,152,320,000	4,361,962	$12,642,848,905,846	$783,308,186,689,846	$2,612,989,440,000	$169,317,586,407,784	$1,438,919
65	551,139,200	$24,470,580,480,000	4,416,179	$12,999,995,880,000	$794,778,771,289,846	$2,645,468,160,000	$173,064,029,162,342	$1,442,065
66	557,905,600	$24,771,008,640,000	4,470,397	$13,362,053,699,077	$806,187,726,230,769	$2,677,946,880,000	$176,790,764,378,737	$1,445,025
67	564,672,000	$25,071,436,800,000	4,524,615	$13,729,022,363,077	$817,530,140,667,692	$2,710,425,600,000	$180,491,265,193,916	$1,447,796
68	571,438,400	$25,371,864,960,000	4,578,833	$14,100,901,872,000	$828,801,103,755,692	$2,742,904,320,000	$184,158,469,542,058	$1,450,377
69	578,204,800	$25,672,293,120,000	4,633,051	$14,477,692,225,846	$839,995,704,049,846	$2,775,383,040,000	$187,784,736,267,940	$1,452,765
70	584,971,200	$25,972,721,280,000	4,687,269	$14,859,393,424,615	$851,109,032,505,231	$2,807,861,760,000	$191,361,797,641,616	$1,454,959
71	591,737,600	$26,273,149,440,000	4,741,487	$15,246,005,468,308	$862,136,176,476,923	$2,840,340,480,000	$194,880,707,979,281	$1,456,957
72	598,504,000	$26,573,577,600,000	4,795,705	$15,637,528,356,923	$873,072,225,720,000	$2,872,819,200,000	$198,331,788,051,059	$1,458,758
73	605,270,400	$26,874,005,760,000	4,849,923	$16,033,962,090,462	$883,912,769,389,539	$2,905,297,920,000	$201,704,564,930,224	$1,460,359
74	612,036,800	$27,174,433,920,000	4,904,141	$16,435,306,668,923	$894,651,396,640,615	$2,937,776,640,000	$204,987,706,910,059	$1,461,761
75	618,803,200	$27,474,862,080,000	4,958,359	$16,841,562,092,308	$905,284,696,628,308	$2,970,255,360,000	$208,168,953,083,896	$1,462,961
76	625,569,600	$27,775,290,240,000	5,012,577	$17,252,728,360,615	$915,807,258,507,692	$3,002,734,080,000	$211,235,037,150,721	$1,463,957
77	632,336,000	$28,075,718,400,000	5,066,795	$17,668,805,473,846	$926,214,171,433,846	$3,035,212,800,000	$214,171,604,972,833	$1,464,750
78	639,102,400	$28,376,146,560,000	5,121,013	$18,089,793,432,000	$936,500,524,561,846	$3,067,691,520,000	$216,963,125,373,246	$1,465,337
79	645,868,800	$28,676,574,720,000	5,175,231	$18,515,692,235,077	$946,661,407,046,769	$3,100,170,240,000	$219,592,793,618,455	$1,465,718
80	652,635,200	$28,977,002,880,000	5,229,449	$18,946,501,883,077	$956,691,908,043,692	$3,132,648,960,000	$222,042,406,986,813	$1,465,891
81	659,401,600	$29,277,431,040,000	5,283,667	$19,382,222,376,000	$966,587,116,707,692	$3,165,127,680,000	$224,292,351,773,490	$1,465,855
82	666,168,000	$29,577,859,200,000	5,337,885	$19,822,853,713,846	$976,342,122,193,846	$3,197,606,400,000	$226,321,281,029,870	$1,465,609
83	672,934,400	$29,878,287,360,000	5,392,103	$20,268,395,896,615	$985,952,013,657,231	$3,230,085,120,000	$228,106,182,277,544	$1,465,153
84	679,700,800	$30,178,715,520,000	5,446,321	$20,718,848,924,308	$995,411,880,252,923	$3,262,563,840,000	$229,622,134,374,875	$1,464,485
85	686,467,200	$30,479,143,680,000	5,500,538	$21,174,212,796,923	$1,004,716,811,136,000	$3,295,042,560,000	$230,842,172,646,612	$1,463,605
86	693,233,600	$30,779,571,840,000	5,554,756	$21,634,487,514,462	$1,013,861,895,461,540	$3,327,521,280,000	$231,737,121,314,132	$1,462,511
87	700,000,000	$31,080,000,000,000	5,608,974	$22,099,673,076,923	$1,022,842,222,384,620	$3,360,000,000,000	$232,422,888,474,868	$1,461,203
88	706,766,400	$31,380,428,160,000	5,663,192	$22,569,769,484,308	$1,031,652,881,060,310	$3,392,478,720,000	$232,142,592,543,271	$1,459,680
89	713,532,800	$31,680,856,320,000	5,717,410	$23,044,776,736,615	$1,040,288,960,643,690	$3,424,957,440,000	$231,394,536,223,094	$1,457,941
90	720,299,200	$31,981,284,480,000	5,771,628	$23,524,694,833,846	$1,048,745,550,289,850	$3,457,436,160,000	$230,399,293,238,163	$1,455,986
91	727,065,600	$32,281,712,640,000	5,825,846	$23,745,682,855,385	$1,057,281,580,074,460	$3,489,914,880,000	$229,136,594,281,969	$1,454,176
92	733,832,000	$32,582,140,800,000	5,880,064	$23,966,670,876,923	$1,065,897,049,997,540	$3,522,393,600,000	$227,584,507,964,869	$1,452,508
93	740,598,400	$32,882,568,960,000	5,934,282	$24,187,658,898,462	$1,074,591,960,059,080	$3,554,872,320,000	$225,719,304,523,268	$1,450,978
94	747,364,800	$33,182,997,120,000	5,988,500	$24,629,634,941,539	$1,083,366,310,259,080	$3,587,351,040,000	$223,515,308,352,958	$1,449,582
95	754,131,200	$33,483,425,280,000	6,042,718	$24,850,622,963,077	$1,092,220,100,597,540	$3,619,829,760,000	$220,944,738,450,183	$1,448,316
96	760,897,600	$33,783,853,440,000	6,096,936	$25,071,610,984,615	$1,101,153,331,074,460	$3,652,308,480,000	$217,977,555,768,883	$1,447,177
97	767,664,000	$34,084,281,600,000	6,151,154	$25,292,599,006,154	$1,110,166,001,689,850	$3,684,787,200,000	$214,581,176,421,217	$1,446,161
98	774,430,400	$34,384,709,760,000	6,205,372	$25,513,587,027,692	$1,119,258,112,443,690	$3,717,265,920,000	$210,720,469,560,545	$1,445,266
99	781,196,800	$34,685,137,920,000	6,259,590	$25,734,575,049,231	$1,128,429,663,336,000	$3,749,744,640,000	$206,357,338,690,799	$1,444,488
100	787,963,200	$34,985,566,080,000	6,313,808	$25,734,575,049,231	$1,137,680,654,366,770	$3,782,223,360,000	$206,357,338,690,799	$1,443,825
TOTALS		$2,173,883,938,560,000		$1,036,203,284,193,230	$1,137,680,654,366,770	$235,014,479,844,324	$206,357,338,690,799	

APPENDIX B
A List of Some Price Controls in the United States

A. HISTORICAL PRICE CONTROLS

- Implementation of a Gold Standard requires the price for an ounce of gold to be fixed in dollar terms.

- During World War I, the United States Food Administration enforced price controls on food. Price controls were also imposed in the US during WWII. The Franklin Roosevelt Administration instituted the OPA (Office of Price Administration) which was phased out after peace had been restored.
- During the Korean War price controls were again established, this time under the OPS (Office of Price Stabilization).

- U.S. President Richard Nixon's Secretary of the Treasury, George Shultz, enacting Nixon's "New Economic Policy," lifted price controls that had begun in 1971. This lifting of price controls resulted in a rapid increase in prices. Price freezes were re-established five months later. The cap on oil and natural gas prices persisted for years finally ending in 1981.

B.   CONTEMPORARY   PRICE   CONTROLS

-   In   2002   The   Federal   Energy   Regulatory Commission set price caps for each megawatt of power   bought.

- Tax policies encourage people to invest into real estate and the stock market and assist in the formation of bubbles. Import Taxes represent price controls, Tax Credits

-Minimum   Wages   &   Rent   Controls.

- Trading Halts: Limit Up/Limit Down. U.S. Securities and Exchange Commission (SEC) and U.S. Commodity Futures Trading Commission (CFTC) regulates trading of securities and commodities, which can be paused for a variety of reasons, such as an upcoming news announcement, to correct an order imbalance, or suspected unusual activity related to price.

- U.S. FATCA law acts as an indirect form of capital controls for Americans by creating prohibitively costly regulatory burdens when foreign banks desire to do business with American clients.
- U.S. Federal Trade Commission and the Department of Justice effectively dictates fair pricing in medicine and pharmaceuticals and enforces it through criminal prosecution. Enforcement of anti-trust laws is another form of price control.

APPENCIX C

A list of scriptures from the Bible that are relevant to welfare.

Deuteronomy 15:7-11 ESV: "If among you, one of your brothers should become poor, in any of your towns within your land that the Lord your God is giving you, you shall not harden your heart or shut your hand against your poor brother, but you shall open your hand to him and lend him sufficient for his need, whatever it may be. Take care lest there be an unworthy thought in your heart and you say, 'The seventh year, the year of release is near,' and your eye look grudgingly on your poor brother, and you give him nothing, and he cry to the Lord against you, and you be guilty of sin. You shall give to him freely, and your heart shall not be grudging when you give to him, because for this the Lord your God will bless you in all your work and in all that you undertake. For there will never cease to be poor in the land. Therefore I command you, 'You shall open wide your hand to your brother, to the needy and to the poor, in your land.'

Acts 20:35 ESV: "In all things I have shown you that by working hard in this way we must help the weak and remember the words of the Lord Jesus, how he himself said, 'It is more blessed to give than to receive.'"

Proverbs 28:27 ESV: "Whoever gives to the poor will not want, but he who hides his eyes will get many a curse."

Philippians 2:2-8 ESV: "Complete my joy by being of the same mind, having the same love, being in full accord and of one mind. Do nothing from rivalry or conceit, but in humility count others more significant than yourselves. Let each of you look not only to his own interests, but also to the interests of others. Have this mind among yourselves, which is yours in Christ Jesus, who, though he was in the form of God, did not count equality with God a thing to be grasped..."

Leviticus 19:9-10 ESV: "When you reap the harvest of your land, you shall not reap your field right up to its edge, neither shall you gather the gleanings after your harvest. And you shall not strip your vineyard bare, neither shall you gather the fallen grapes of your vineyard. You shall leave them for the poor and for the sojourner: I am the Lord your God."

James 2:14-24 ESV: "What good is it, my brothers, if someone says he has faith but does not have works? Can that faith save him? If a brother or sister is poorly clothed and lacking in daily food, and one of you says to them, "Go in peace, be warmed and filled," without giving them the things needed for the body, what good is that? So also faith by itself, if it does not have works, is dead. But someone will say, "You have faith and I have works." Show me your faith apart from your works, and I will show you my faith by my works."

2 Thessalonians 3:6-12 ESV: "Now we command you, brothers, in the name of our Lord Jesus Christ, that you keep away from any brother who is walking in idleness and not in accord with the tradition that you received from us. For you yourselves know how you ought to imitate us, because we were not idle when we were with you, nor did we eat anyone's bread without paying for it, but with toil and labor we worked night and day,

that we might not be a burden to any of you. It was not because we do not have that right, but to give you in ourselves an example to imitate. For even when we were with you, we would give you this command: If anyone is not willing to work, let him not eat."

Romans 15:1-2 ESV: "We who are strong have an obligation to bear with the failings of the weak, and not to please ourselves. Let each of us please his neighbor for his good, to build him up."

Luke 12:33 ESV: "Sell your possessions, and give to the needy. Provide yourselves with moneybags that do not grow old, with a treasure in the heavens that does not fail, where no thief approaches and no moth destroys."

Romans 14:1 ESV: "As for the one who is weak in faith, welcome him, but not to quarrel over opinions."

Luke 16:13 ESV: "No servant can serve two masters, for either he will hate the one and love the other, or he will be devoted to the one and despise the other. You cannot serve God and money."Hebrews 13:15-16 ESV: "Through him then let us continually offer up a sacrifice of praise to God, that is, the fruit of lips that acknowledge his name. Do not neglect to do good and to share what you have, for such sacrifices are pleasing to God."

Romans 12:17-21 ESV: "Repay no one evil for evil, but give thought to do what is honorable in the sight of all. If possible, so far as it depends on you, live peaceably with all. Beloved, never avenge yourselves, but leave it to the wrath of God, for it is written, "Vengeance is mine, I will repay, says the Lord." To the contrary, "if your enemy is hungry, feed him; if he is thirsty, give him something to drink; for by so doing you will heap burning coals on his head." Do not be overcome by evil, but overcome evil with good."

Luke 21:1-4 ESV: "Jesus looked up and saw the rich putting their gifts into the offering box, and he saw a poor widow put in two small copper coins. And he said, "Truly, I tell you, this poor widow has put in more than all of them. For they all contributed out of their abundance, but she out of her poverty put in all she had to live on."

Luke 3:12-14 ESV: "Tax collectors also came to be baptized and said to him, "Teacher, what shall we do?" And he said to them, "Collect no more than you are authorized to do." Soldiers also asked him, "And we, what shall we do?" And he said to them, "Do not extort money from anyone by threats or by false accusation, and be content with your wages.""

Jeremiah 29:11-14 ESV: "For I know the plans I have for you, declares the Lord, plans for welfare and not for evil, to give you a future and a hope. Then you will call upon me and come and pray to me, and I will hear you. You will seek me and find me, when you seek me with all your heart. I will be found by you, declares the Lord, and I will restore your fortunes and gather you from all the nations and all the places where I have driven you, declares the Lord, and I will bring you back to the place from which I sent you into exile."

Acts 2:42-46 ESV: "And they devoted themselves to the apostles' teaching and the fellowship, to the breaking of bread and the prayers. And awe came upon every soul, and many wonders and signs were being done through the apostles. And all who believed were together and had all things in common. And they were selling their possessions and belongings and distributing the proceeds to all, as any had need. And day by day, attending the temple together and breaking bread in their homes, they received their food with glad and generous hearts..."

Mark 12:31 ESV: "The second is this: 'You shall love your neighbor as yourself.' There is no other commandment greater than these."

Proverbs 14:21 ESV: "Whoever despises his neighbor is a sinner, but blessed is he who is generous to the poor."

Leviticus 19:18 ESV: "You shall not take vengeance or bear a grudge against the sons of your own people, but you shall love your neighbor as yourself: I am the Lord."

Colossians 3:12-14 ESV: "Put on then, as God's chosen ones, holy and beloved, compassionate hearts, kindness, humility, meekness, and patience, bearing with one another and, if one has a complaint against another, forgiving each other; as the Lord has forgiven you, so you also must forgive. And above all these put on love, which binds everything together in perfect harmony."

2 Corinthians 9:7 ESV: "Each one must give as he has decided in his heart, not reluctantly or under compulsion, for God loves a cheerful giver.

Matthew 9:10-13 ESV: "And as Jesus reclined at

table in the house, behold, many tax collectors and sinners came and were reclining with Jesus and his disciples. And when the Pharisees saw this, they said to his disciples, "Why does your teacher eat with tax collectors and sinners?" But when he heard it, he said, "Those who are well have no need of a physician, but those who are sick. Go and learn what this means, 'I desire mercy, and not sacrifice.' For I came not to call the righteous, but sinners."

Matthew 6:31-34 ESV: "Therefore do not be anxious, saying, 'What shall we eat?' or 'What shall we drink?' or 'What shall we wear?' For the Gentiles seek after all these things, and your heavenly Father knows that you need them all. But seek first the kingdom of God and his righteousness, and all these things will be added to you. "Therefore do not be anxious about tomorrow, for tomorrow will be anxious for itself. Sufficient for the day is its own trouble."

James 2:8 ESV: "If you really fulfill the royal law according to the Scripture, "You shall love your neighbor as yourself," you are doing well.'

Hebrews 13:1-3 ESV: "Let brotherly love continue. Do not neglect to show hospitality to strangers, for thereby some have entertained angels unawares. Remember those who are in prison, as though in prison with them, and those who are mistreated, since you also are in the body."

Philippians 3:18-19 ESV: "For many, of whom I have often told you and now tell you even with tears, walk as enemies of the cross of Christ. Their end is destruction, their god is their belly, and they glory in their shame, with minds set on earthly things."

John 13:34-35 ESV: "A new commandment I give to you, that you love one another: just as I have loved you, you also are to love one another. By this all people will know that you are my disciples, if you have love for one another."

Luke 6:38 ESV: "Give, and it will be given to you. Good measure, pressed down, shaken together, running over, will be put into your lap. For with the measure you use it will be measured back to you."

Luke 6:31 ESV: "And as you wish that others would do to you, do so to them."

Mark 12:28-31 ESV: "And one of the scribes came up and heard them disputing with one another, and seeing that he answered them well, asked him, "Which commandment is the most important of all?" Jesus answered, "The most important is, 'Hear, O Israel: The Lord our God, the Lord is one. And you shall love the Lord your God with all your heart and with all your soul and with all your mind and with all your strength.' The second is this: 'You shall love your neighbor as yourself.' There is no other commandment greater than these."

Matthew 25:31-46 ESV: "When the Son of Man comes in his glory, and all the angels with him, then he will sit on his glorious throne. Before him will be gathered all the nations, and he will separate people one from another as a shepherd separates the sheep from the goats. And he will place the sheep on his right, but the goats on the left. Then the King will say to those on his right, 'Come, you who are blessed by my Father, inherit the kingdom prepared for you from the foundation of the world. For I was hungry and you gave me food, I was thirsty and you gave me drink, I was a stranger and you welcomed me,..."

Matthew 7:12 ESV: "So whatever you wish that others would do to you, do also to them, for this is the Law and the Prophets."

Matthew 5:5-9 ESV: "Blessed are the meek, for they shall inherit the earth. Blessed are those who hunger and thirst for righteousness, for they shall be satisfied. Blessed are the merciful, for they shall receive mercy. Blessed are the pure in heart, for they shall see God. Blessed are the peacemakers, for they shall be called sons of God."

Proverbs 28:20 ESV: "A faithful man will abound with blessings, but whoever hastens to be rich will not go unpunished."

Psalm 37:21 ESV: "The wicked borrows but does not pay back, but the righteous is generous and gives;"

Romans 13:8-10 ESV: "Owe no one anything, except to love each other, for the one who loves another has fulfilled the law. For the commandments, 'You shall not commit adultery, You shall not murder, You shall not steal, You shall not covet,' and any other commandment, are summed up in this word: 'You shall love your neighbor as yourself.' Love does no wrong to a neighbor; therefore love is the fulfilling of the law."

Luke 18:9-14 ESV: "He also told this parable to some who trusted in themselves that they were righteous, and treated others with contempt: "Two men went up into the temple to pray, one a Pharisee and the other a tax collector. The Pharisee, standing by himself, prayed thus: 'God, I thank you that I am not like other men, extortioners, unjust, adulterers, or even like this tax collector. I fast twice a week; I give tithes of all that I get.' But the tax collector, standing far off, would not even lift up his eyes to heaven, but beat his breast, saying, 'God, be merciful to me, a sinner!' I tell you that this tax collector, rather than the other, went home justified before God. For all those who exalt themselves will be humbled, and those who humble themselves will be exalted."

Luke 16:10-12 ESV: "One who is faithful in a very little is also faithful in much, and one who is dishonest in a very little is also dishonest in much. If then you have not been faithful in the unrighteous wealth, who will entrust to you the true riches? And if you have not been faithful in that which is another's, who will give you that which is your own?"

Luke 10:25-28 ESV: 'And behold, a lawyer stood up to put him to the test, saying, "Teacher, what shall I do to inherit eternal life?" He said to him, "What is written in the Law? How do you read it?" And he answered, "You shall love the Lord your God with all your heart and with all your soul and with all your strength and with all your mind, and your neighbor as yourself." And he said to him, "You have answered correctly; do this, and you will live."'

Mark 9:35 ESV: "And he sat down and called the twelve. And he said to them, "If anyone would be first, he must be last of all and servant of all."

Matthew 23:1-33 ESV: "Then Jesus said to the crowds and to his disciples, "The scribes and the Pharisees sit on Moses' seat, so practice and observe whatever they tell you—but not what they do. For they preach, but do not practice. They tie up heavy burdens, hard to bear, and lay them on people's shoulders, but they themselves are not willing to move them with their finger. They do all their deeds to be seen by others. For they make their phylacteries broad and their fringes long"

Matthew 20:25-28 ESV: "But Jesus called them to him and said, "You know that the rulers of the Gentiles lord it over them, and their great ones exercise authority over them. It shall not be so among you. But whoever would be great among you must be your servant, and whoever would be first among you must be your slave, even as the Son of Man came not to be served but to serve, and to give his life as a ransom for many."

Matthew 18:21-35 ESV: "Then Peter came up and said to him, "Lord, how often will my brother sin against me, and I forgive him? As many as seven times?" Jesus said to him, "I do not say to you seven times, but seventy times seven. "Therefore the kingdom of heaven may be compared to a king who wished to settle accounts with his servants. When he began to settle, one was brought to him who owed him ten thousand talents. And since he could not pay, his master ordered him to be sold, with his wife and children and all that he had, and payment to be made. At this the servant fell on his knees before him. 'Be patient with me,' he begged, 'and I will pay back everything.' The servant's master took pity on him, canceled the debt and let him go."

Matthew 18:10 ESV: "See that you do not despise one of these little ones. For I tell you that in heaven their angels always see the face of my Father who is in heaven.

Matthew 16:26 ESV: "For what will it profit a man if he gains the whole world and forfeits his soul? Or what shall a man give in return for his soul?"

Matthew 7:15-20 ESV: "Beware of false prophets, who come to you in sheep's clothing but inwardly are ravenous wolves. You will recognize them by their fruits. Are grapes gathered from thornbushes, or figs from thistles? So, every healthy tree bears good fruit, but the diseased tree bears bad fruit. A healthy tree cannot bear bad fruit, nor can a diseased tree bear good fruit. Every tree that does not bear good fruit is cut down and thrown into the fire."

Matthew 6:24 ESV: "No one can serve two masters, for either he will hate the one and love the other, or he will be devoted to the one and despise the other. You cannot serve God and money."

Matthew 6:14-15 ESV: "For if you forgive others their trespasses, your heavenly Father will also forgive you, but if you do not forgive others their trespasses, neither will your Father forgive your trespasses."

Matthew 6:1-7 ESV: "Beware of practicing your righteousness before other people in order to be seen by them, for then you will have no reward from your Father who is in heaven. "Thus, when you give to the needy, sound no trumpet before you, as the hypocrites do in the synagogues and in the streets, that they may be praised by others. Truly, I say to you, they have received their reward. But when you give to the needy, do not let your left hand know what your right hand is doing, so that your giving may be in secret. And your Father who sees in secret will reward you. "And when you pray, you must not be like the hypocrites. For they love to stand and pray in the synagogues and at the street corners, that they may be seen by others. Truly, I say to you, they have received their reward."

Matthew 5:43-48 ESV: "You have heard that it was said, 'You shall love your neighbor and hate your enemy.' But I say to you, Love your enemies and pray for those who persecute you, so that you may be sons of your Father who is in heaven. For he makes his sun rise on the evil and on the good, and sends rain on the just and on the unjust. For if you love those who love you, what reward do you have? Do not even the tax collectors do the same? And if you greet only your brothers, what more are you doing than others? Do not even the Gentiles do the same?"

Matthew 5:43-45 ESV: "You have heard that it was said, 'You shall love your neighbor and hate your enemy.' But I say to you, Love your enemies and pray for those who persecute you, so that you may be sons of your Father who is in heaven. For he makes his sun rise on the evil and on the good, and sends rain on the just and on the unjust."

Matthew 5:42 ESV: "Give to the one who begs

from you, and do not refuse the one who would borrow from you."

Matthew 5:38-40 ESV: "You have heard that it was said, 'An eye for an eye and a tooth for a tooth.' But I say to you, Do not resist the one who is evil. But if anyone slaps you on the right cheek, turn to him the other also. And if anyone would sue you and take your tunic, let him have your cloak as well."

Matthew 5:7 ESV: "Blessed are the merciful, for they shall receive mercy."

Zechariah 7:9 ESV: "Thus says the Lord of hosts, Render true judgments, show kindness and mercy to one another,"

Micah 3:11-12 ESV: Its heads give judgment for a bribe; its priests teach for a price; its prophets practice divination for money; yet they lean on the Lord and say, "Is not the Lord in the midst of us? No disaster shall come upon us." Therefore because of you Zion shall be plowed as a field; Jerusalem shall become a heap of ruins, and the mountain of the house a wooded height.

Isaiah 58:10-11 ESV: If you pour yourself out for the hungry and satisfy the desire of the afflicted, then shall your light rise in the darkness and your gloom be as the noonday. And the Lord will guide you continually and satisfy your desire in scorched places and make your bones strong; and you shall be like a watered garden, like a spring of water, whose waters do not fail.

Isaiah 46:3-4 ESV: "Listen to me, O house of Jacob, all the remnant of the house of Israel, who have been borne by me from before your birth, carried from the womb; even to your old age I am he, and to gray hairs I will carry you. I have made, and I will bear; I will carry and will save.

Proverbs 24:29 ESV: Do not say, "I will do to him as he has done to me; I will pay the man back for what he has done."

Deuteronomy 24:14 : "Do not take advantage of a hired worker who is poor and needy, whether that worker is a fellow Israelite or a foreigner residing in one of your towns."

APPENDIX D

A short list of all of the social welfare benefits that all people, rich, poor and middle class in developed countries have utilized in their lifetime. Given that we are all the recipients of welfare, the only question is why not simply increase it in a way that does not represent a direct burden to anyone. This list contains references to government programs that are specific to the United States but that can also be equated to similar programs in other developed countries.

NOTE: The only thing that is not on this list is the use of public lands upon which to live, hunt, grow food and gather water. This is the fundamental thing that the government inadvertently prevents people today from being able to do, unless an individual has, obtains or inherits sufficient wealth and/or land ownership.

A. Default Facilities: Existing before most people today where born:
Use of roads; Use of sidewalks and traffic lights; Use of public parks; Use of public water fountains; Use of public libraries; Public Schools; Fire Departments; Police Departments; Orphanages; The Military; Border Control Agents (that keep others out of our country); Courts; Prisons; Use of Churches

B. Programs Based: The wealthy benefit from the following programs by virtue of the fact that there are not poor people living in the streets, adding to crime rates, getting sick, spreading disease and dying and thus creating many more problems.

Medical Care (Medicaid, Medicare), Public Housing, Subsidized Rent (Section 8 Housing), Food Stamps, Monetary Assistance; Social Security Income; Disability payments for handicapped; Medical Clinics;

BIBLIOGRAPHY

THE EVOLUTION OF MONEY

2014, The History Channel television show, "Big History" speaks about why early man valued gold.

In the December, 2009 issue of National Geographic, A tribe called The Hadza, by Michael Finkel.

http://www.details.com/culture-trends/career-and-money/200907/meet-the-man-who-lives-on-zero-dollars?currentPage=4

http://www.indians.org/articles/native-american-money.html   (on Native American Money)

The Aldrich-Vreeland Act of 1908, provided for emergency currency issues during crises. The act also established the National Monetary Commission to search for a long-term solution to the nation's banking and financial problems.

HOW DOES NEW MONEY GET CREATED

https://www.youtube.com/watch?v=w2tKg3E53DM   (Vsauce,   How much Money is on Earth? Commodity Money, Representative Money, Fiat Money-let it be done, Tinkerbell Effect)

http://www.thetrailofgreen.com/

http://www.frbsf.org/education/teacher-resources/datapost/macroeconomics/money-supply

http://www.forbes.com/fdc/welcome_mjx.shtml

http://www.businessweek.com/news/2014-03-05/china-21-trillion-debt-load-seen-swelling-on-14-economic-plan

http://theeconomiccollapseblog.com/archives/it-is-now-mathematically-impossible-to-pay-off-the-u-s-national-debt

http://en.wikipedia.org/wiki/Money_creation

HOW MUCH USD IS IN EXISTANCE TODAY

http://data.worldbank.org/indicator/CM.MKT.LCAP.CD   (total   market capitalization)

http://www.gurufocus.com/stock-market-valuations.php (total market capitalization) http://www.businessinsider.com/wfe-world-stock-market-capitalization-2013-12 (total market capitalization of the globe)

http://www.federalreserve.gov/pubs/bulletin/2000/1200lead.pdf (% of total outstanding securities held by mutual funds in 2000 20% of equities and 10% of bonds)

http://www.ici.org/pdf/2013_factbook.pdf (total worldwide assets invested in mutual funds)

http://www.frbsf.org/education/files/MoneySupply_rev_2014-07-07.pdf (US Federal Reserve M1,M2)

http://research.stlouisfed.org/fred2/series/USAWFPNA (working age people in USA, 2012)

http://www.federalreserve.gov/releases/iba/fboshr.htm (Total Loans VS Total Deposits)

http://www.infowars.com/cfr-floats-free-money/ the CFR, About giving money away to curb inflation.

WHAT HAPPENS WHEN ONE COUNTRY BUYS ANOTHERS DEBT

http://www.usgovernmentdebt.us/

http://www.foxbusiness.com/economy-policy/2014/01/16/china-now-owns-record-1317t-us-government-debt/

http://usgovinfo.about.com/od/moneymatters/ss/How-Much-US-Debt-Does-China-Own.htm

THE REAL CAUSES OF INFLATION

http://www.huffingtonpost.com/2013/05/30/reinhart-rogoff-debunked_n_3361299.html
(Economists argue over the relationship between government debt and economic health)

http://www.farmcollector.com/farm-life/u-s-farmers-during-great-depression.aspx#axzz3GhvuXfWX

IN DEFENSE OF WELFARE

http://www.therichest.com/rich-list/world/poorest-countries-in-the-world/2/

http://anitra.net/homelessness/columns/anitra/eightmyths.html

http://www.huffingtonpost.com/2014/02/20/food-stamps-celebrities_n_4824405.html

A MORE PRACTICAL MODEL BASED ON THE STOCK MARKETS

http://www.nytimes.com/2013/11/17/magazine/switzerlands-proposal-to-pay-people-for-being-alive.html?pagewanted=all&_r=0

http://dealbook.nytimes.com/2014/06/22/an-employee-dies-and-the-company-collects-the-insurance/?_php=true&_type=blogs&_r=0

http://www.monbiot.com/2014/09/02/someone-elses-story/ system justification becomes stronger when social and economic inequality is extreme.

HOW THIS SYSTEM CAN BE IMPLEMENTED TODAY WITHOUT THE GOVERNMENT

http://dealbook.nytimes.com/2014/06/22/an-employee-dies-and-the-company-collects-the-insurance/?_php=true&_type=blogs&_r=0

A SHORT LIST OF PEOPLE WHO AGREE ABOUT THE VALUE AND NATURE OF MONEY

https://www.minneapolisfed.org/publications_papers/pub_display.cfm?id=3787&

http://www.forbes.com/sites/nathanlewis/2014/07/24/on-the-path-to-a-better-monetary-system-bretton-woods-didnt-fail-because-of-the-balance-of-payments/

http://www.forbes.com/sites/moneybuilder/2014/07/03/book-review-steve-forbes-money/

http://www.economist.com/blogs/democracyinamerica/2013/11/government-guaranteed-basic-income

http://www.adamsmith.org/blog/welfare-pensions/the-ideal-welfare-system-is-a-basic-income/

http://www.huffingtonpost.com/david-vognar/the-case-for-a-guaranteed_b_5568347.html

http://www.economonitor.com/dolanecon/2014/01/27/a-universal-basic-income-conservative-progressive-and-libertarian-perspectives-part-3-of-a-series/

http://www.salon.com/2013/10/11/rather_than_savage_cuts_switzerland_considers_star_trek_economics/

http://www.reuters.com/article/2013/10/04/us-swiss-pay-idUSBRE9930O620131004

http://www.infowars.com/cfr-floats-free-money/   the   CFR,   About
giving money away to curb inflation.

http://www.foreignaffairs.com/articles/141847/mark-blyth-and-eric-
lonergan/print-less-but-transfer-more

QUESTIONS AND ANSWERS (Q&A)

http://www.businessinsider.com/rich-and-famous-people-who-were-
homeless-2014-8?op=1

http://anitra.net/homelessness/columns/anitra/eightmyths.html

http://www.huffingtonpost.com/2014/02/20/food-stamps-
celebrities_n_4824405.html

http://www.alternet.org/story/156234/exposing_how_donald_trump_
really_made_his_fortune%3A_inheritance_from_dad_and_the_gove
rnment's_protection_mostly_did_the_trick

http://en.wikipedia.org/wiki/Rationing_in_Cuba

http://www.mps.gov.cn/n16/n84147/n84196/3837042.html

http://lawandborder.com/faq-new-china-visa-law/

http://www.dailyfinance.com/2013/05/05/the-5-states-with-no-sales-
tax/

http://www.dpw.state.pa.us/foradults/cashassistance/S_001312

http://berkleycenter.georgetown.edu/essays/religious-freedom-in-
cuba

http://www.openbible.info/topics/welfare

OTHER RELEVANT SOURCES

http://www.economicpolicyjournal.com/2014/11/warning-bank-
deposits-will-soon-no.html
Money becomes even less tangible

http://tinyurl.com/m6jnkyv
Woody Harrelson 'Ethos Time to Unslave Humanity

https://www.facebook.com/events/758689310865362/
Governments moving towards new system

http://www.nytimes.com/2014/10/26/us/law-lets-irs-seize-accounts-
on-suspicion-no-crime-required.html?_r=2
Goverment Controls Money, No Due Process

http://www.local10.com/news/police-charge-90yearold-man-2-pastors-with-feeding-the-homeless/29510268
Prevented from Feeding the Homeless

http://computationalculture.net/article/what-do-metrics-want
The Desire for More

http://www.washingtonpost.com/blogs/wonkblog/wp/2012/09/19/heres-why-the-47-percent-argument-is-an-abuse-of-tax-data/
Poor people about the taxes they pay

http://www.ijreview.com/2014/11/203641-2-chart-new-definition-fair-share-20-americans-pay-almost-100-everything/
Rich people about the taxes they pay

http://www.huffingtonpost.com/2014/11/05/jackie-speier-homelessness_n_6102336.html?cps=gravity
Congress Woman Sleeps in Homeless Shelter

http://www.infoplease.com/timelines/voting.html
History of Voting Rights in US

http://www.washingtontimes.com/news/2014/apr/21/americas-oligarchy-not-democracy-or-republic-unive/
America an Oligarchy, Princeton and Northwest Universities

http://www.free2pray.info/5founderquotes.html
Religion and Education

http://newscenter.berkeley.edu/2010/03/05/wendybrown/
Public Education

http://www.econ.brown.edu/econ/sthesis/IanPapers/paper1.html
Democracy and Education

http://en.wikipedia.org/wiki/Student_loan_default_in_the_United_States
7 Million default student loans

http://www.forbes.com/sites/specialfeatures/2013/08/07/how-the-college-debt-is-crippling-students-parents-and-the-economy/
Student Debt Crisis

http://www.newyorkfed.org/research/staff_reports/sr668.pdf
New York Fed on Student Loans (17% delinquency rate, $1Trillion USD)

http://www.bbc.com/news/world-us-canada-30275026

Texas Closing Prisons in Favor of Rehab

http://ccia.eu/
Community Currencies

http://www.neweconomics.org/
Economic Think Tank

http://www.bitcoin.org
About BitCoin

ABOUT THE AUTHOR

The author, Eric Majors, is an expert in financial market analysis and algorithms, with a Bachelors of Science in Electrical Engineering from the University of Colorado. Mr. Majors is a former U.S. Registered Investment Advisor and business owner who worked with the CIA. He has served as an officer and director of a number of publicly traded companies and as a principal of an international investment banking firm. He is an expert on global currencies and was the principal inventor of Trade Series Management Theory and the associated TSM financial market software systems. Mr. Majors is a certified Consciousness Coach, business advisor, speaker, teacher and author. Mr. Majors is the author of "Financial Markets And Technical Analysis" (2005), "Dot Money" (2014), Dot Money the Global Currency Reserve, Questions & Answers" 2015 Edition and "Dealing with Loss for Believers and Everyone" (2015).

From 2010 to 2013, Mr. Majors spent over 3 years in a U.S. Federal Prison after pleading guilty in 2009 to charges stemming from his work with the CIA and Insider Trading. As a result of the diverse experiences and international exposure that led to his incarceration Mr. Majors is now able to share his unique prospective on life and the global financial markets. He does so from the viewpoint of an insider who speaks candidly and openly.

For more information about this book and Eric Majors visit: www.EricMajors.com

ABOUT "DOT MONEY" THE BOOK

Dot Money may be the most important book of our time. It has the potential to transform the world and the lives of every individual for the better. This book explores the creation and use of money, global monetary systems, and our preconceived ideas of money. Then it reveals how ordinary people can take control of the money system today, making it work for them as an alternative to just working to make ends meet. Dot Money is more than a book it is a movement.

Dot Money reveals the next step in the evolution of global economics and shows us how to solve the most important problems of our time. This book has the potential to enable us to overcome poverty, and increase the standard of living for every human being regardless of their current resources, education, race, religion, health, geographic location, political or social affiliations.

For more information please visit:
www.DotMoneyBook.com

www.ingramcontent.com/pod-product-compliance
Lightning Source LLC
Chambersburg PA
CBHW070548200326
41519CB00012B/2154